D1604838

A
Through
the
Bible
Reading
Program

Victory Chapel Community Church Library

Edwin V. Hayden
Roy W. McKinney
Gary H. Hall
Thomas D. Thurman

 STANDARD PUBLISHING

Cincinnati, Ohio

3076

The material appearing on pp. 4, 5, 76, and 77 is condensed from lessons in TRAINING FOR SERVICE: *A Survey of the Bible,* revised © 1983, The Standard Publishing Company.

Most Scripture quotations are taken from the NEW INTERNATIONAL VERSION of the Bible, Copyright © 1978 by the New York International Bible Society. Used by permission.

ISBN: 0-87239-647-9

Copyright © 1983, The STANDARD PUBLISHING Company, Cincinnati, Ohio.
A division of STANDEX INTERNATIONAL Corporation. Printed in U.S.A.

A Through the Bible Reading Program

Chances are you've never read all the way through the Bible. You probably know it would be good for you, and you mean to do it someday. You might read sections of it for your Bible-school lesson each week, or read along with the Scripture reading from the pulpit, but to read the entire Bible through seems a little too ambitious a project right now.

Or maybe you've started to read through the Bible and kept it up for a few weeks or months, but then began to fall behind until it got too difficult to catch up again—probably somewhere in Leviticus.

Or perhaps you *have* read through the Bible before and you already know how much you benefited from it, and you want to do it again—maybe in a different order this time.

Here's where this program will help. It's a little different than other Bible reading schedules. The readings are arranged chronologically—that is, in the order in which the events took place in history, not the order of the books of the Bible. Instead of reading four separate accounts of the life of Jesus, for example, you can read one account in a harmony of all four Gospels.

A second unique feature of this program is that you have only five readings scheduled per week, and two days off. Although the five readings are listed Monday through Friday, you can actually schedule your readings for the week however you want to. As you complete each day's reading, check off the box beside it. With two days off per week, you're less likely to fall far behind schedule and quit.

The reading and study of parts of the Bible is helpful, but you're missing something if you haven't read the Bible through. You're missing the whole *story* of the Bible—the context of the teachings of Jesus and Paul, and of the stories of faith and courage that you learned as a child.

The Bible is the story of how God dealt with the people He created;

how He remained faithful to His people even though they turned from Him again and again;

how God, from the very beginning, began to prepare the world for His own coming as a man—knowing all the while that His own people would reject Him and put Him to death.

The meaning of that death, and of the resurrection that followed, is the happy ending, that part of the Bible story most important to us today.

The Old Testament

The two main divisions in the Bible are the Old Testament and the New Testament.

The books of the Old Testament fall naturally into four groups: Law, History, Poetry, and Prophecy. The names given to the four divisions give a general idea of what is in them, but no division is limited to one kind of literature. The books of law contain also history, poetry, and prophecy; the books of prophecy have much history and poetry. Nor is their order in the Old Testament necessarily the same as the chronological order in which they were written. Job, a book of poetry, may well be the oldest book of the Bible. The books of prophecy cover times from before the fall of the northern kingdom of Israel until the times after the return of Judah from exile, over three hundred years later.

Law

The books of law are the first five books of the Bible. They trace God's dealings with mankind from "the beginning" through the flood of Noah's time, through the beginning of the Hebrew nation in Abraham, Isaac, and Jacob, through their escape from Egypt and their wandering in the wilderness, to the time when Moses died and his people were ready to enter the promised land with Joshua as their leader.

All this history provides the setting in which God gave the Hebrew people the law that fills a large part of this group of books. This is sometimes called the Jewish law or the Old Testament law. The best-known parts of it are the Ten Commandments (Exodus 20:3-17).

History

The books of history begin with Joshua and end with Esther. They record much of the preparation for the coming of Christ.

These books cover about a thousand years, from the conquest of the promised land in about 1400 B.C. to the end of the Old Testament in about 400 B.C. Naturally, they cannot tell everything that happened, but they record the course of history in a general way and show clearly the effects of following God's law and ignoring it. The books deal principally with the Hebrews because it was through them that the Christ was to come.

Poetry

The books of poetry have a large influence on the sacred music and worship even of the present day. The lyric poetry of the Hebrews was at its height nearly a thousand years before the lyrics of Horace. The writer of Ecclesiastes discussed the world's vanity five hundred years before Socrates talked in Athens. Some of the psalms are nearly a thousand years older than Ovid, yet today they are sung by more people than ever before. Other ancient poetry is known to only a few scholars, but the poetry of the Bible is cherished in millions of devout hearts.

Prophecy

The prophetic books include some of the finest literature ever written in any language. The student of the Bible, however, is not chiefly interested in literary value. His chief question is this: Are these books really messages from God, and if so, what is God saying to us in them? These books do bring us one convincing proof of the inspiration of both the Old and New Testaments, and of the divinity of Christ.

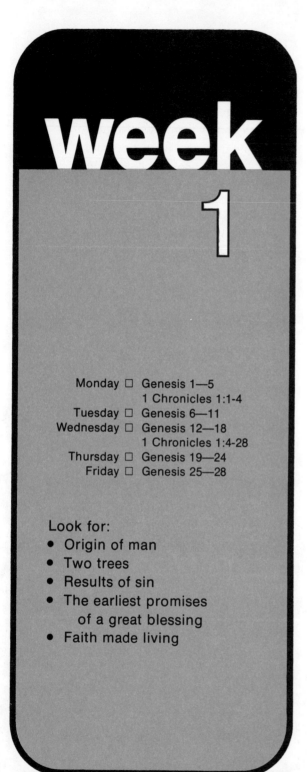

week 1

Monday ☐ Genesis 1—5
1 Chronicles 1:1-4
Tuesday ☐ Genesis 6—11
Wednesday ☐ Genesis 12—18
1 Chronicles 1:4-28
Thursday ☐ Genesis 19—24
Friday ☐ Genesis 25—28

Look for:
- Origin of man
- Two trees
- Results of sin
- The earliest promises of a great blessing
- Faith made living

Genesis is a book of origins.

It presents the origin of physical existence, of man, and of the race through which God would unfold His plan of eternal redemption. On the dark side it describes the advent of sin into the human race.

These concepts are fundamental to the Christian's belief today. If we look upon Genesis as merely being Jewish mythology it becomes difficult, if not impossible, to explain the mission of Christ to the world. The doctrine of origins in Genesis is essential to the Biblical view of man and Christ.

"What Is Man?"

Man, according to scientific philosophy, is *only* a combination of his environment, genes, and the chemical reactions of his physical body. Death is simply a discontinuation of these chemical reactions. Genesis teaches that man is created in the image of God. Man is physical but he is also spiritual. His faithfulness is rewarded by eternity with God.

No view of man is complete without taking into account the devastating influence of sin. After man sinned in the garden, he went into a state of spiritual decline. Man's heart became continually evil in God's sight, so God destroyed the earth with a flood. The purpose of that flood was twofold: to destroy sin and to save righteous Noah.

Noah marked a new beginning in the relationship between God and man. This account should give us insight into the terrible results of sin and the value of faithfulness to God.

The Golden Text of the Old Testament

After Noah and the Tower of Babel, men began to scatter over the face of the earth. In Ur, located in the Mesopotamian valley, there lived a man of great faith. God called Abram to leave his home and move toward the promised land. As Abram entered the land, God made some great promises to him: He would bless Abram, make his name great, and bless all the families of the earth through his descendant (Genesis 12:1-3). The rest of the Bible is a story of the fulfillment of these promises made to Abram.

Faith without outward expression is dead and useless. A living faith must be expressed by keeping the law of love. Abraham loved God, but he also loved his son Isaac. No doubt it was a crushing blow to the heart of Abraham when God commanded him to sacrifice his only son. Though all human logic cried out against such an act, faith demanded submission to the will of God.

Faith won out. Abraham set out to do exactly as God had commanded him. In the end, Abraham was called a friend of God.

Ordinary People

The people we are reading about are no different from ourselves. They were ordinary people facing the same weaknesses and failures that we experience today. The story of Jacob should vividly illustrate this point. He took advantage of his brother, his father, and his uncle Laban, sometimes with deliberate deception. But God used him to become the father of the twelve tribes of Israel.

Jacob began badly but ended well. His story should be a comfort to us today.

week 2

Monday ☐ Genesis 29—31
Tuesday ☐ Genesis 32—36
           1 Chronicles 1:28—2:2
Wednesday ☐ Genesis 37—41
Thursday ☐ Genesis 42—45
Friday ☐ Genesis 46—50

Look for:
- Love and deception
- Wrestling with an angel
- Dreams and interpretations
- A Hebrew ruler in Egypt
- God's people in Egypt

A Divided Household

While Jacob was living in Padan-Aram, he became the father of eleven sons. Benjamin was born later near Bethlehem. These sons became the heads of the twelve tribes of Israel. There was contention in the home of Jacob because he loved Rachel more than Leah.

This chaotic condition is reflected in the names given to each son. If your Bible has footnotes you can find a history of the upheaval in Jacob's home life written in the meanings of each of the sons' names. The name of Judah, whose tribe produced the Messiah, means "Praise."

After his return to the promised land, Jacob made a mistake that is common today. He, maybe unintentionally, showed favoritism to Joseph. This is understandable, since Joseph was the son of Rachel, his beloved. The other sons responded with bitter hatred for Joseph; they seized him and sold him to a caravan going to Egypt. The brothers then had the problem of explaining Joseph's disappearance to their aging father. The truth had to be kept from Jacob at all costs. So they brought Joseph's blood-stained coat to Jacob and deceived him into thinking that his son had been killed by wild animals. And so Jacob, who had similarly deceived his own father years before, was now deceived by his children.

God's Providence

When Joseph arrived in Egypt, he was sold to Potiphar and became his head household slave. Due to his rejection of the improper advances made by Potiphar's wife and her false accusations, Joseph was imprisoned for two years. Was God unjust to let such heinous things happen to His faithful servant? You might answer "yes" if you're looking only from the short-range viewpoint. But when seen from God's perspective of His ultimate purpose, His providence is clearly seen. God was using the machinations of men to achieve His purposes for His people Israel. God wanted Joseph in Egypt to be His agent to save Israel through the seven-year drought that was coming.

An interesting encounter took place when Jacob's sons went to Egypt to buy food. Joseph, their brother, was the man they had to see. When this man accused them of being spies (he did not reveal his identity to them until later), they began to rationalize the cause of their plight as being punishment for the evil done to their brother. They had to live with the burden of their conscience.

The end result of Joseph's position in Egypt was the preservation of the people of God. By the time the brothers had gotten to Egypt, Joseph had ascertained this fact. Surely many questions had arisen in the mind of Joseph while he sat in prison for two years. Now all the pieces fell into place. God was with him through it all. This knowledge should be great comfort to all whose trust is placed in the Lord.

After the death of Jacob the brothers began to fear retribution from Joseph. He reassured them by stating his faith in God's providential care. He told them, "You intended to harm me, but God intended it for good . . ." (50:20). This does not excuse the brothers from their evil deed but it does show the spiritual depth of the heart of Joseph.

Let us not make the mistake of judging too quickly God's concern for us when calamities take place in our lives.

9

week 3

Monday ☐ Job 1—3
Tuesday ☐ Job 4—9
Wednesday ☐ Job 10—15
Thursday ☐ Job 16—23
Friday ☐ Job 24—31

Look for:
- The cause of Job's troubles
- A desire for death
- "If a man dies, will he live again?"
- Longing for God
- The cry of the innocent

It is possible that the book of Job is the oldest book in the Bible. Situations in the book reflect social conditions that were prevalent during the time of Abraham.

Job was an extraordinary man. He was "the greatest man among all the people of the East" (1:3). The context indicates that this statement is in reference to his great wealth. Yet he was a man of deep spiritual character and true faith in God. This combination is rare among men. Though wealthy, Job looked upon his relationship with God as his most valuable asset.

Why?

Job fell from a state of health and wealth to one of a disease-ridden pauper. If he was such a spiritual and submissive individual, why did he have to endure such horrible suffering?

The explanation comes from a most surprising direction: These things befell him simply because he was a friend of God. Satan, before God, challenged the validity of Job's faith, suggesting that Job remained faithful only because God had given him so much. God gave Satan permission to test the faith of His friend.

"In all this, Job did not sin by charging God with wrongdoing" (1:22). It is easy to maintain a stance of faithfulness when matters of life are favorable. To maintain faithfulness when all of life collapses is a different matter. How many times do Christians say, "If God loves me like He says He does, why do these things happen to me?" It is possible that "these things" happen because God does love. In all his problems, not once did Job accuse God of being false to him. With Abraham, Job was a man of sustaining faith.

With Friends Like These . . .

Job's friends expressed some questionable friendship in their attempts to comfort him. They suggested that to improve this lot he must resolve the cause of his problems. The premise of their argument was that punishment was the result of sin. Man sins and God punishes. Therefore, Job must confess and repent of his sin and then his punishment would be removed.

Job insisted that he had not sinned, and therefore his misfortunes were not the result of his sins. In this Job was right. His friends had taken a valid Biblical principle and misapplied it. All misfortune is *not* the result of sin. The only reasonable attitude is to maintain faith regardless of what happens, be it good or bad.

Amazingly, Job maintained his faith even under the pressure of the arguments used by his friends. Eliphaz said, "do not despise the discipline of the Almighty" (5:17), when Job bemoaned the fact that he had been born. Bildad's "comforting" words were, "God does not re-

ject a blameless man" (8:20). Job could only reply that he did not understand but he was not an overt sinner. Zophar, adding his bit of wisdom, said, "Know then that God exacts of you less than your guilt deserves" (11:6; KJV). The pathos of Job's reply can be summed up in, "I, a just and blameless man, am a laughingstock."

The pressures from these arguments led Job to earnestly desire the day of his death. We, too, may be tempted at times to state the reasons why such things happen to individuals, but this is a foolish pastime. The magnitude of Job's faith is shown by his refusal to sin against God, even under such circumstances as these.

week 4

Monday ☐ Job 32—37
Tuesday ☐ Job 38—42
Wednesday ☐ Exodus 1—6
Thursday ☐ Exodus 7—11
Friday ☐ Exodus 12—15

Look for:
- The all-powerful, all-knowing God
- The birth of Moses
- The Lord's Passover
- A psalm of victory

God Ends the Debate

Elihu, the young upstart theologian, now had his chance to correct Job's misconceptions. His arguments are based on God's omniscience and omnipotence. How could a mere man like Job call into question the punishment of God? This would be a telling argument if we did not already know the real reason for Job's calamities.

Then God himself came to Job's rescue, but the only answer God would give made a strong demand on the faith of Job. In an overwhelming barrage of questions and challenges to Job, He left no doubt that He is an all-knowing and all-powerful God. If He could create the behemoth (possibly the hippopotamus) and the leviathan (possibly the crocodile), He could care for any problem that confronted Job.

With this Job was satisfied. The end result was that Job enjoyed more and greater blessings than he had before his faith had been tested.

Reluctant Deliverer

Years after the death of Joseph, the people of Israel were made slaves in Egypt. They cried out to God under the bitter bondage they were suffering at the hands of the Egyptians.

In response to their pleading, God raised up Moses, the great deliverer. He had spent forty years in Midian and was reluctant to accept the call of God to this tremendous task. Moses argued that he was slow of speech and therefore not qualified. God gave him Aaron to be his spokesman and the two brothers entered Egypt, demanding of Pharaoh that he let the people go. The day of salvation had arrived; deliverance was at hand!

Well, not yet. Pharaoh's reaction was to make the burdens of the people even less bearable than they were before. They were to make their usual quota of bricks, but now they had to gather their own straw with which to make them. The people began to complain; Moses was not bringing deliverance, but only making their burdens greater.

At that point Moses was discouraged, to say the least. "If the *Israelites* will not listen to me, why would Pharaoh listen?" he complained to God. But God had other plans. Since Pharaoh would not listen to reason, the plagues were sent upon the Egyptians. As the plagues progressed, they became more and more destructive to the Egyptians until finally, the horror of the death of the firstborn fell on them. At midnight Pharaoh called in Moses, demanding that the Israelites leave Egypt.

The Salvation of the Lord

On that night of death, the Lord passed over the houses of the faithful who had put the blood of the sacrificial lamb on their doors. The Passover Feast was begun as a perpetual reminder of this great deliverance.

The elements of this feast were the lamb, unleavened bread, and bitter herbs. The lamb was the sacrifice that made deliverance possible, the bitter herbs indicated the bitterness of the Egyptian bondage, and the unleavened bread told of the haste in which they had left the land of bondage. The lamb of Passover was a type of Christ. Those under the blood of the lamb that night were delivered from death.

When the people of Israel arrived at the Red Sea, their faith faltered again as they saw the army of Egypt coming behind them. Moses reassured them with those magnificent words, "Fear ye not, stand still, and see the salvation of the Lord" (Exodus 14:13, KJV).

Now, truly, deliverance would be wrought. By crossing the Red Sea, Israel would pass from bondage into freedom. Paul looked back on this event and used it as a type of Christian baptism (1 Corinthians 10:1, 2).

week 5

Monday ☐ Exodus 16—20
Tuesday ☐ Exodus 21—24
Wednesday ☐ Leviticus 25
Exodus 25—27
Thursday ☐ Exodus 28—30
Friday ☐ Exodus 31:1—35:29

Look for:
- The mountain of revelation
- The Ten Commandments
- A golden calf
- Bitter waters
- The tabernacle erected

Sevens

About six weeks before they arrived at Mt. Sinai, God instituted the Sabbath for His people. It was to be a day of rest, commemorating God's creation rest and perpetually reminding Israel that God had delivered them from bondage in Egypt.

The laws concerning the sabbatical year and the year of jubilee are given in Leviticus 25. Every seventh year the land was to lie idle. Nothing that grew would be harvested. God promised that He would bless the sixth year so that enough could be harvested to last three years. This would demand total dependence on the promises of God. In the year of jubilee all land would revert back to its original owner: "The land must not be sold permanently, because the land is mine and you are but aliens and my tenants" (Leviticus 25:23). This was a perpetual lesson that what they owned was not theirs, but God's. A spirit of self-sufficiency is hard to develop under these circumstances.

Mt. Sinai

When Israel arrived at Sinai, they had an astounding experience. The mountain was wrapped in smoke, lightning flashed, trumpet blasts were heard, and the mountain quaked. From the cloud-covered mountain the voice of God was heard calling Moses to come up and meet Him there. It is small wonder that the people trembled.

When God spoke the Ten Commandments to Moses, He introduced them by saying, "I am the Lord your God, who brought you out of Egypt, out of the land of slavery" (Exodus 20:2). Because He delivered them, they were to obey Him. Their obedience was to come from a spirit of gratitude for what God had done for them.

The Ten Commandments pointed Israel toward the proper relationship to God and to their fellowman. Jesus taught that obedience to these commandments was an expression of love to both God and man.

Other Laws

After giving the commandments, God revealed additional laws. The law of Moses was both for civil and religious life; Israel's form of government was a theocracy.

Home structure was strongly emphasized in the law. A child that struck or cursed his parents was put to death (Exodus 21:15, 17). By our modern standards this seems extremely excessive, but the Old Testament approach to crime was either capital punishment or restitution. In all the law there is no mention of imprisonment as punishment.

One law is misunderstood today. It is said, "An eye for an eye" (21:23-25) is an act of revenge, but such is not the case. This law was for the protection of the poor. If a rich man disregarded the rights of a poor man and arbitrarily knocked out his eye, the poor man could take his case before the elders. If the rich man was found guilty, his eye was knocked out. This law assured the social protection of all strata of their society.

Exodus 28 described the attire to be worn by the priests. Their robes, breastplates, and turbans are described. On their turbans they were to wear a golden plate inscribed, "Holy to the Lord" (28:36). This summarizes the function of the priests. They were to offer sacrifices for the sins of the people. Christ, our great High Priest, functions to make us holy to the Lord.

week

6

Monday ☐ Exodus 35:30—40:38
Tuesday ☐ Leviticus 8, 9
Numbers 8
Numbers 7
Wednesday ☐ Leviticus 1—5
Thursday ☐ Leviticus 6, 7, 10, 11
Friday ☐ Leviticus 12—15

Look for:
- Great craftsmen of God
- Led by a cloud
- Regulations for the priests
- Dedication of the tabernacle
- Clean and unclean food

In Exodus 40:17 we are told that Moses erected the tabernacle on the first day of the *second* year. A whole year had passed since the Exodus began. We can hardly imagine the tremendous difficulties that Moses must have experienced moving such a large multitude through the barren Sinai wilderness.

The Tabernacle

God gave detailed instructions for the building of the tabernacle and its appointments. The court was to have the altar of sacrifice and the laver. Behind the first curtain of the tabernacle was the Holy Place that contained the table of the presence, the altar of incense, and the golden lampstand. Behind the second curtain, commonly known as the veil, was the Most Holy Place, in which was found the ark of the covenant. On the lid of the ark were two cherubim. Their outspread wings overshadowed the mercy seat. Contained in the ark were the tablets of stone of the Ten Commandments.

Portrayed here at the mercy seat was the essence of true religion. On the great Day of Atonement the high priest sprinkled the sacrificial blood on the mercy seat. The commandments written on stone were a witness against the sins of the people (Deuteronomy 31:26). The blood-soaked lid "covered" this testimony against their sins. From this grew the concept "to cover guilt" or "to make atonement." It was here that reconciliation between God and man was accomplished. This was a type of the blood of Christ, who is the propitiation, or atonement, for our sins.

A close association is made between the mercy seat and God's presence. In Leviticus 16:2 God said, "I will appear in the cloud upon the mercy seat" (KJV). After Moses had erected the tabernacle at God's instruction we are told, "Then the cloud covered the Tent of Meeting, and the glory of the Lord filled the tabernacle" (Exodus 40:34). Because of what was accomplished at the mercy seat, the covering of sin, the glory of God's presence was made available to His people.

The Hebrews served a copy or shadow of the heavenly sanctuary (Hebrews 8:5). Moses, having seen the pattern of the heavenly tabernacle (Exodus 25:40), was to build an earthly copy of it. Christ serves as priest in the heavenly tabernacle. His ministry is far superior to that of Aaron. We, today, have the privilege of belonging to this superior priesthood of Christ.

Unholy Fire

Moses also gave instructions concerning the priests and Levites. Nadab and Abihu, sons of Aaron, were Levitical priests, but their burning of incense was not in accordance to the commands of the Lord (Leviticus 10:1). As a result fire fell from the Lord and devoured them.

We may constantly be tempted to vary from the prescribed statements of Scripture, but the story of Nadab and Abihu teach the lesson that God's commands should be obeyed without deviation.

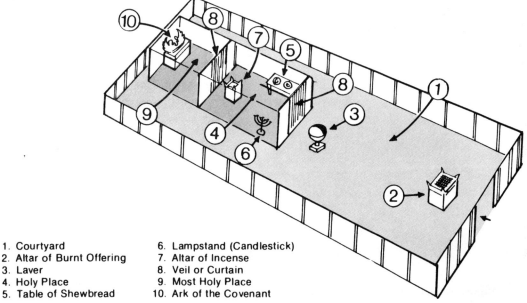

1. Courtyard
2. Altar of Burnt Offering
3. Laver
4. Holy Place
5. Table of Shewbread
6. Lampstand (Candlestick)
7. Altar of Incense
8. Veil or Curtain
9. Most Holy Place
10. Ark of the Covenant

week 7

Monday ☐ Leviticus 16—18
Tuesday ☐ Leviticus 19—22
Wednesday ☐ Leviticus 23, 24, 26, 27
Thursday ☐ Numbers 1—3
Friday ☐ Numbers 4—6

Look for:
- Why blood is sacred
- "You shall be holy"
- Religious festivals
- The punishment for blasphemy
- Benediction (Numbers 6)

Scapegoat

"The goat will carry on itself all their sins to a solitary land" (Leviticus 16:22). On the Day of Atonement the priest placed his hands on the head of a goat and confessed over him all the iniquities and sins of Israel. The goat was then led into the wilderness and released.

The scapegoat became a type of Christ. In Isaiah 53:4, 6 we read, "Surely he took up our infirmities and carried our sorrows . . . the Lord has laid on him the iniquity of us all."

The types found in the tabernacle worship are highly Messianic. The altar of sacrifice, the scapegoat, the mercy seat, other appointments of the tabernacle, and the priestly functions all point forward to the advent of the Messiah and His ministry of reconciliation. Judaism is a unique religion. It is the only one in the history that looked to the day that it would be replaced by a new and entirely different religious system—the day when the Messiah would come.

Priests and Laws

The Levitical priests were to act on behalf of men in relation to God, but they were instructed to offer sacrifice for themselves before they sacrificed for the people (Leviticus 16:11). They were to realize that they had weaknesses just as the people did, and empathize with the erring Israelites.

God bound these laws and regulations on the people of Israel for their own good, not merely to show His absolute authority over them. His purpose, as stated in Leviticus 18:5,

was, "Keep my decrees and laws, for the man who obeys them will live by them. I am the Lord." Arbitrary as they may seem at times, the ordinances of the Lord are designed for man's good.

"Which Is the Greatest Commandment?"

This was a question put to Jesus by a skeptical lawyer. Jesus told him that it was to love the Lord your God with all your heart, soul, and mind. The individual who loves God with this intensity will devote himself to keeping every command of the Word of God.

Jesus continued by saying that another law was like it: you shall love your neighbor as yourself. We are to hold our neighbor in high esteem and respect. Jesus also taught us to forgive in the same manner that we want Him to forgive us (Matthew 6:12). Jesus said that the whole law depends on these two commands.

Despite the harshness of its prescribed punishments, and its "eye-for-an-eye" reputation, the Old Testament law itself condemns a vengeful attitude: "Do not seek revenge or bear a grudge against one of your people, but love your neighbor as yourself. I am the Lord" (Leviticus 19:18).

Many define orthodoxy as proper faith toward God. Biblical orthodoxy is proper faith toward God that finds expression in a love for others.

Nazirites

Number 6 introduces the law of the Nazirite. This was an individual separated to the Lord, one who had dedicated himself to a special purpose or task. Throughout the history of Israel are accounts of men who were separated to the Lord. God works His ways through men dedicated to Him.

week 8

Monday ☐ Numbers 9—12
Tuesday ☐ Numbers 13, 14
        Deuteronomy 1:19-46
Wednesday ☐ Numbers 15:1—20:13
Thursday ☐ Numbers 20:14—24:25
Friday ☐ Numbers 25—29

Look for:
- Complaints and punishments
- Moses, God's special servant
- Two faithful spies
- Swallowed by the earth
- A donkey speaks

Rebellions: Miriam and Aaron

Moses had to bear the burden of constant rejection and discontent from every quarter.

"Moses has married a Cushite," his brother and sister criticized. Their real problem was that God had placed Moses in a position of leadership over them. Hadn't God spoken through them as well as Moses?

When God heard, He called them before Him. In His chastisement of them God pointed out that Moses occupied a special position. Indeed, God spoke to prophets in dreams and visions, but with Moses He would speak face to face (Numbers 12:8), a special privilege because of special responsibility. Because God spoke directly to Moses, the law occupied a unique position in the structure of the Old Testament.

Ten Spies

After leaving Sinai, Moses led the Israelites toward the promised land. Upon arrival at Kadesh-Barnea twelve men were sent to spy out the land. After forty days they returned with a mixed report. The land flowed with milk and honey, they said, but the cities had walls that reached to heaven and there were giants dwelling in the land. Ten of the spies suggested that the people turn back because of the insurmountable difficulties before them. Joshua and Caleb, exhibiting great faith in God, encouraged the people to go into the land and conquer it.

The Israelites listened to the unfaithful spies rather than to Joshua and Caleb. Because of their faithlessness, God told the Israelites that they would wander in the wilderness one year for each day the spies had spent in the promised land. At that point they changed their minds and tried to go in and take the land, but it was too late. They were defeated.

The Israelites experienced a sad period in their history. They wandered forty years in a wilderness so barren that life could hardly be sustained. God's mercy was still with them, though. He gave them manna to eat and kept their clothing from deteriorating.

Korah

Korah and his friends ridiculed Moses, saying, "You have gone too far! The whole community is holy, every one of them, and the Lord is with them. Why then do you set yourselves above the Lord's assembly?" (Numbers 16:3). They were accusing Moses of the very sin that had overcome them, that of selfish ambition.

The Lord vindicated Moses in a manner that left no question as to who was the leader of Israel. The 250 followers of Korah were told to come before the Lord with their censers burning. God sent fire from Heaven, and the only thing that remained were the smoking censers.

God, through Moses, told Eleazar to beat the bronze censers into plates and to cover the altar of sacrifice with them. The bronze altar was a perpetual reminder to the Israelites not to rebel against Moses and the Lord.

Balaam

When Moses entered into Transjordan, Balak king of Moab sent for Balaam to come and curse the Israelites. He offered great treasures for this service. When Balaam attempted to curse them, though, he could only bless them because of God's influence over him. Balak then refused to pay what he had promised. In a spirit of vengeance, Balaam enticed some of the Israelites to commit idolatry with the people of Peor. Moses led those who were still faithful in an attack on the Midianites. In that battle, Balaam was killed (Numbers 31:8, 16). Balaam paid the penalty for the sins of greed and rebellion against God's will.

week

9

Monday ☐ Numbers 30—32
Deuteronomy 2, 3
Tuesday ☐ Numbers 33—36
Wednesday ☐ Deuteronomy 1:1-18
Deuteronomy 4, 5
Thursday ☐ Deuteronomy 6—9
Friday ☐ Deuteronomy 10—14

Look for:
- The death of Balaam
- Settlement in Transjordan
- The exodus and the
journey of Israel
- Why the law?
- Writing on stone

Sea of Reeds

Numbers 33 is a resume of the Exodus out of Egypt. Here events are presented in their chronological order. This brings up an interesting point of criticism.

Many writers contend that "Red Sea" should be translated "Reed Sea." The reason, in many cases, is to imply that the sea was small and shallow and that the Israelites could have waded across without any miraculous intervention on God's part.

There are two grievous errors in this reasoning. First, the Egyptian soldiers must have been rather inept to drown in knee-deep water. The second has to do with the movement of the Israelites. After they crossed the sea, they went three days' journey into the wilderness and camped at Etham, followed by Marah, then Elim. Then Moses said they "camped by the Red Sea" (Numbers 33:10). Either the "Reed Sea" was extremely large or the Israelites were poor travelers.

It is best to accept the narrative as written: God parted the waters of the Red Sea and the Israelites crossed on dry land.

Edom and Meribah

On the way to Moab, Moses appealed to Edom to let Israel pass through their land. Edom refused, but God told Moses not to raise the sword against their brothers. Esau, the brother of Jacob, was the progenitor of the Edomites. Though Israel was God's people, He still had concern for others.

Another important event is associated with Meribah. There was no water in the wilderness, and the people complained to Moses and Aaron. God heard their murmuring and told Moses to give the people water by striking a rock with his rod. Moses made a tragic error in losing his temper and striking the rock without giving God the glory. As a result, God told him that he and Aaron would not enter the promised land.

We can sympathize with Moses for losing his patience, for he had heard the bickering and complaining of the Israelites for nearly forty years. It might be argued that the penalty was too severe for the transgression, but the lesson to be learned is the enormity of the results of sin.

Teaching

"Hear, O Israel: the Lord our God, the Lord is one" (Deuteronomy 6:4) is one of the most amazing statements ever penned by man. It came out of a religious environment that was totally polytheistic. Like a thunderbolt out of the blue came that marvelous statement of Moses: there is one God and He is our Lord. The idea that Israel got her concepts about deity from her religious

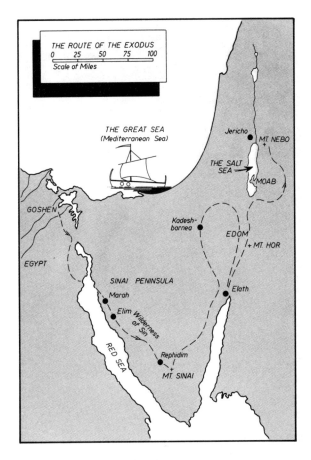

neighbors is absolutely contrary to historical fact.

The Pentateuch places great emphasis on the education of children. After Moses gave the Shema (Deuteronomy 6:4) he instructed parents to teach the law to their children. They were to talk about the law in their houses, when they walked in the way, when they lay down at night and when they arose in the morning. Not only were they to be extensive in the amount of time spent teaching; they were to do it diligently (Deuteronomy 6:6, 7). The primary responsibility of instruction was placed on the home.

week

10

Monday ☐ Deuteronomy 15—19
Tuesday ☐ Deuteronomy 20—25
Wednesday ☐ Deuteronomy 26—28
Thursday ☐ Deuteronomy 29:1—
31:29
Friday ☐ Deuteronomy 31:30—
34:12
Psalm 90

Look for:
- A hole in the ear
- The king's book
- Show no pity
- Go to Mount Ebal
- God's covenant people

The Second Law

While on the plains of Moab awaiting Israel's entrance into the promised land, Moses wrote the book of Deuteronomy. Its historical narrative covers a period of forty years. The name means "the second law," but it is far more than a mere restating of the law as given in other books of the Pentateuch. Moses reviewed his people's experiences so that they would not make the same mistakes that they made in the past. As they were about to enter a new phase in their life as a nation, Moses wanted to encourage them to strengthen their faith and commitment that they might enjoy life in their new land in a way that God intended.

Prophets and Monuments

One such source of help was the institution of the office of prophet (Deuteronomy 18:9-22). The idolatrous inhabitants of Canaan would tempt Israel to go into the ways of error. Moses exposed and condemned such degrading practices as burning children as sacrifices to pagan gods. God's people were not to indulge in these abominations. If an Israelite was proven guilty of such an offense on the word of more than one witness, he was to be stoned to death.

To counteract these evil influences, God would raise up prophets like Moses who would declare to them the revelation of God. The office of prophet was Messianic in character; it pointed to Christ, and He was the fulfillment of it (Acts 3:17-23).

Anticipating their entrance into the promised land, Moses instructed the Israelites to go to Mount Ebal and Mount Gerizim (Deuteronomy 27:1-8). There Joshua was to read them the blessings and the curses of the law. They were to set up large stones, covering them with plaster. They were to write "very plainly" the words of the law on the plaster monument. It would be there for all to see. This monument was to be a perpetual reminder that the law of God was the constitution of their new nation.

The Death of Moses

The thirty-fourth chapter of Deuteronomy poses a problem in the minds of many people. Since it describes the death of Moses, it is logical to conclude that Moses did not write it. Many negative critics argue that since Moses did not write this chapter, he did not write any of the Pentateuch. This is an extremely thin argument; other qualified men could have written this addition to the book of Deuteronomy. Joshua is a likely candidate, since he enjoyed the inspiration of the Holy Spirit.

It is a commonly held belief that Moses was buried on Mount Nebo. The Scriptures plainly state that he was buried in the valley of the land of Moab (Deuteronomy 34:6). The exact location of the burial remained the secret of God. In this the Lord's wisdom is evident. The Israelites, who had a tendency toward idolatry, might well have made his tomb a shrine for worship.

week 11

Monday ☐ Joshua 1—6
Tuesday ☐ Joshua 7—10
Wednesday ☐ Joshua 11—15
Thursday ☐ Joshua 16—21
Friday ☐ Joshua 22—24

Look for:
- Be strong and of good courage
- The scarlet cord
- Joshua deceived
- "O sun, stand still"
- A word of farewell

Parting of the Waters

Under their new leader, Joshua, Israel marched to the east bank of the Jordan and prepared to enter the promised land. When the feet of the priests carrying the ark of the covenant touched the waters of the Jordan, the waters rose in a heap upstream at Adam. Israel crossed over the Jordan on dry ground. When the waters of the Red Sea parted for Moses, there was no question in the minds of Israel that Moses was God's chosen leader. In like fashion the parting of the Jordan was God's stamp of approval upon Joshua as the new leader of Israel (Joshua 4:14).

Battles

The first town to be captured was Jericho. After the report of the spies that the men of Jericho were in a state of chaotic fear, the attack began. It was the most unique battle in the history of the world, and the city fell easily into the hands of Israel.

The next city to be attacked was Ai. Joshua confidently sent a small force to eradicate it. When the dust of battle had settled, Israel was running in retreat. In his prayer to God, Joshua expressed total frustration. "Ah, Sovereign Lord, why did you ever bring this people across the Jordan . . ." (Joshua 7:7). God's answer was that there was sin in Israel. All the booty from Jericho was to be devoted to the Lord, but a man named Achan had kept a mantle and some silver and gold for himself. When

Joshua had determined that Achan was the culprit, he ordered Achan stoned to death. The counterattack on Ai brought victory to Joshua.

After Joshua read the blessings and the curses of the law to the people at Mount Ebal, his conquest of Canaan continued. Israel overwhelmed the Amorites with the miraculous help of the Lord. As the Amorites fled toward their homeland, God caused great hailstones to fall on them. Joshua then prayed for the sun to stand still until Israel could completely conquer its enemy. The Hebrew text says the sun stayed at the half (in other words, at noon) and remained there for about a day.

After Joshua conquered the southern lands (he took the best land first) he turned north. The tribes of northern Canaan formed a confederacy to fight against Israel, but this worked for Israel's benefit; one victory would settle the issue. Joshua let some of the cities stand as a future line of defense against attacks from the north.

Judgment on Canaan

In the cities conquered by Joshua, the total populations were slaughtered. At first glance this appears to be vicious on the part of Joshua and vindictive on the part of God, but the real reason lies in a promise made by God to Abraham (Genesis 15:16). Israel's conquest of Canaan had a dual purpose. The Canaanites were to be punished because of the enormity of their sins. Their moral standards had deteriorated to the level that they were indulging in human sacrifice. The other purpose was to provide the people of God a land in which to live.

At the close of his life, Joshua encouraged the Israelites to be faithful to the Lord that they might live long in the land. As the old faithful warrior pleads for loyalty from the Israelites, our hearts, too, are lifted by those stirring words. "Choose for yourselves this day whom you will serve . . . but as for me and my household, we will serve the Lord" (Joshua 24:15).

week
12

Monday ☐ Judges 1—5
Tuesday ☐ Judges 6—8
Wednesday ☐ Judges 9—12
Thursday ☐ Judges 13—17
Friday ☐ Judges 18—21

Look for:
- The pattern of cycles
- A deadly hospitality
- Putting out a fleece
- A strange engagement party
- A message of outrage

Cycles

The book of Judges could well be called the book of cycles. The recurring theme of the book is a cycle of sin, oppression, deliverance by a judge, and back into sin again. The amazing feature of this period is the persistent patience of God. To see God forgiving time and time again in the face of the Israelites' constant return to sin should reaffirm our appreciation of His grace.

These events did not occur over a short measure of time. The period between Othniel and Samson is 390 years, an unstable period between the firm control of Joshua and the reign of King Saul. Ideally speaking, the period represented the type of civil structure that God wanted for His people. It was a pure theocracy. The people depended totally on God for their national and spiritual life.

Because of Israel's sin the Lord let Moab prevail over them for 18 years. In response to the cry of the people, God raised up Ehud to deliver them. Ehud made an appointment with Eglon to give him a tribute. Ehud, being left-handed, had hidden his sword under his clothes on his right side. While they were alone, Ehud drew his sword in his left hand and struck down Eglon. With the death of Eglon, the Israelites rallied behind

Ehud and gained their freedom. They had learned their lesson, at least temporarily. The land had peace for 80 years.

Deborah and Barak

Barak appeared to be a warrior that did not have much self-confidence. The Lord through Deborah, the judge, summoned him to fight against the armies of Jabin, the Canaanite king. Barak agreed to go to battle only if Deborah went with him. She agreed, but told him that because of this a woman would get the glory for killing Sisera, commander of the enemy armies.

Sisera came into the plains of Esdraelon with an innumerable army and 900 chariots of iron against the foot soldiers of Israel. The Israelites won the battle after the Lord caused the river Kishon to overflow its banks and the chariot wheels to sink into the mud. Barak gained the victory. Sisera escaped, but eventually was killed by Jael, fulfilling Deborah's prophecy.

Jephthah

His mother was a harlot and his father was Gilead; due to his checkered background he was driven from his home into the land of Tob. At the time the Israelites were under Ammonite oppression, and, desperate for a leader, they called Jephthah to lead them into battle. Before going to the battlefield, Jephthah vowed that if the Lord would give him victory, he would offer as a burnt offering whatever came out of his house to meet him when he returned home.

The victory was won and the first person to meet him on his return was his daughter. With a troubled soul, he explained to his daughter the vow under which he was bound. She asked her father for two months to bewail the fact that she had never married. He granted her wish before fulfilling his vow.

Many explain this vow to mean that Jephthah intended to give his daughter in service at the tabernacle, but this is suggesting more than the text will allow.

week 13

Monday ☐ Ruth 1—4
Tuesday ☐ 1 Samuel 1:1—4:1a
Wednesday ☐ 1 Samuel 4:1b—8:22
Thursday ☐ 1 Samuel 9—12
Friday ☐ 1 Samuel 13:1—16:13

Look for:
- "Your God will be my God"
- A grateful mother
- "Give us a king!"
- To obey is better than sacrifice
- A young man in the king's court

The Architect of the Kingdom

It was under Samuel's judgeship that the monarchy was introduced and established in Israel. This was a critical period in the history of Israel, and Samuel was God's man for the hour.

The life of Samuel had the right kind of beginning. His mother was a faithful, godly woman. She brought him to the tabernacle to be raised by Eli, the priest, in the service of the Lord. It is small wonder that Samuel became a great man of God.

Eli was a good man who had one obvious failure; his sons are described as "wicked men." They abused their position as priests by treating the offering of the Lord with contempt. Because of this situation a man of God told Eli that his family would lose their place of service in the priesthood. It was at this point that the Lord turned to Samuel.

The Capture of the Ark

Israel went out to do battle against the Philistines, and brought the ark of the covenant with them into the camp. If the ark was there, surely God's presence would be with them also, they reasoned. Yet in the battle not only were the Philistines victorious, but they even captured the ark. (Also in the battle, Eli's sons Hophni and Phinehas were killed, fulfilling God's judgment on Eli's house.)

When the Philistines captured the ark, they got more than they bargained for. In every city where the ark was taken, plague and disease fell on the people. The Philistines wisely sent the ark back to Israel.

The ark was first taken to Bethshemesh. A large number of men there, to satisfy their curiosity, looked into the ark. God slew them for this act, because it was contrary to the ordinances concerning the ark. The ark was then sent to Kiriath-jearim, and it stayed there at least 20 years under the care of Eleazar.

Israel's First King

Samuel had the same problem as Eli; his sons were worthless. Not wanting Samuel's sons to succeed him as judge, the people asked for a king. Samuel warned the people of the troubles that having a king would bring, especially the burden of taxation, but the people still wanted a king.

The Lord chose Saul to be the first king of Israel. At the time Saul was well-qualified for the task. He was humble almost to a fault. Saul's first act was to rally Israel to fight the Ammonites when they attacked Jabesh-gilead. He won the victory and the loyalty of the people.

Saul's downfall began when he unlawfully offered sacrifice at Gilgal. Samuel promised to come to offer sacrifice before Saul fought with the Philistines. When Samuel delayed coming, Saul took it on himself to offer the sacrifice. Then Samuel arrived, and he told Saul that because

of his disobedience the kingdom would be taken from him.

Samuel later instructed Saul to destroy the Amalekites, but Saul brought some cattle and king Agag back from the battle with him. He told Samuel he had brought the cattle back as a sacrifice to the Lord. Samuel's reply was, "To obey is better than sacrifice, and to heed is better than the fat of rams" (1 Samuel 15:22).

In every case of disobedience not once did Saul express repentance, but always tried to rationalize his actions. Justifying obedience always ends in downfall.

week 14

Monday ☐ 1 Samuel 17:1—18:1
1 Samuel 16:14-23
1 Samuel 18:2—19:24
Psalm 59
Tuesday ☐ 1 Samuel 20—22
Psalm 52
Psalms 34, 56, 57, 142
Wednesday ☐ 1 Samuel 23—26
Psalm 54
Thursday ☐ 1 Samuel 27, 29, 30
1 Chronicles 12:1-22
1 Samuel 28, 31
1 Chronicles 10
Friday ☐ 2 Samuel 1—4

Look for:
- "I come in the name of the Lord"
- "Is Saul also among the prophets?"
- Howling dogs prowling the city
- Friends devoted to each other
- Lamentation over Saul

One of the most popular stories in the Old Testament is that of David and Goliath. It is a story of unconquerable faith in the face of insurmountable odds. When David arrived at the battlefield, Goliath was ridiculing the armies of Israel, challenging some champion to come out to fight against him. David's response was, "Who is this uncircumcised Philistine, that he should defy the armies of the living God?" (1 Samuel 17:26) Rejecting the armor of Saul, he went out to face Goliath equipped with a sling and his trust in God. The victory belonged to David.

Before this spectacular event David had played his harp in the royal court to soothe the troubled heart of King Saul.

Saul and David

After slaying Goliath, David returned to Saul's court. But this time as David played, Saul remembered the song he had heard the women singing the day before: "Saul has slain his thousands, and David his tens of thousands" (1 Samuel 18:7). Jealousy and fear controlled his mind and it triggered his efforts to destroy David. David had to run for his life. It was a period of despondency for David as Saul tried time and again to kill him. At one point David said to Jonathan, "As the Lord lives . . . there is only a step between me and death" (1 Samuel 20:3). David was being tempered in the crucible of adversity so that he might become a concerned and compassionate king.

32

As David fled the efforts of Saul to kill him, he displayed a remarkable trait of character. Twice he had opportunity to kill King Saul. On both occasions he refused to harm the king. When reprimanded by his friends his reply was, "The Lord forbid that I should do such a thing to my master, the Lord's anointed" (1 Samuel 24:6). David's respect for the king, who was chosen and anointed by the Lord, was greater than his concern for his own life.

The Philistines gathered their forces to fight against Israel. Saul was at a loss as to what move to make. God had ceased to speak to Saul because of his disobedience, and Samuel, in the meantime, had departed this life. In desperation Saul went to a medium in an effort to contact Samuel.

The message Samuel had for the distraught king was devastating. Saul was told that the kingdom was taken away from him, Israel would fall into the hands of Philistia, and he and his sons would join Samuel on the morrow. The lesson came crashing home to Saul that sin brings total and complete destruction.

The Death of Saul

When the battle was joined Saul's sons were killed by Philistine swords. When Saul saw that he was surrounded by the enemy he asked his armor-bearer to run him through with the sword so that he would not have to suffer the disgrace of being captured. When his armor-bearer refused, Saul fell on his own sword. The Philistines, as an act of humilia-

tion, hung his body on the wall of Bethshan. Valiant men from Jabesh-gilead came and removed his body, burying him at Jabesh. So ended the life of a man who had great potential but fell because of disobedience.

An Amalekite came to David's camp with the news of the death of Saul. Hoping to gain favor from David he said he had killed Saul upon Saul's request. David's response was, "Your own mouth testified against you when you said, 'I killed the Lord's anointed'" (2 Samuel 1:16). David called one of his soldiers to put him to death.

When the news of Saul's death was spread throughout Israel, the tribe of Judah came to Hebron and made David their king. The tribes to the north made Ish-bosheth, son of Saul, their king. Two brothers, Baanah and Rechab, assassinated him and brought his head to David. As a reward for such a dastardly deed David had his soldiers put them to death. Conditions were now such that David could become king of all Israel.

week 15

Monday ☐ 2 Samuel 5, 6
1 Chronicles 11:1-9;
12:23—15:29
Tuesday ☐ 1 Chronicles 16
Psalm 24
Psalms 15, 96, 105, 106
Wednesday ☐ 2 Samuel 7, 8
1 Chronicles 17, 18
Psalms 60, 108
Thursday ☐ 1 Chronicles 11:10-47
2 Samuel 22
Psalm 18
Friday ☐ 1 Chronicles 19
2 Samuel 9—12
Psalm 51

Look for:

- The city of David
- Dancing in the streets
- A psalm of thanksgiving
- Kindness to Saul's family
- A parable of guilt

David Sets Up His Throne

David reigned over Judah seven and one half years from the city of Hebron. The elders of Israel came to him after the death of Ish-bosheth and anointed him king over all the nation. His reign lasted for forty years, seven over Judah and 33 over all Israel. David decided to establish his throne in Jerusalem.

In Jerusalem the citadel on Mount Zion was well fortified. The Jebusites taunted David, saying they could defend their city with the blind and lame. David gained entrance by having his soldiers go up the water shaft that came up inside the walls of the fortification. With the city now in his hands, David built a palace there to live in, and Jerusalem became known as the city of David. Then he brought the ark of the covenant to Jerusalem.

The Ark

At least forty years had passed from the time the Philistines returned the ark until David determined to bring it into Jerusalem. David gathered 30,000 leading men of Israel to accompany the ark on its journey. They carried the ark on an oxcart.

The whole method of moving the ark was contrary to the law of Moses. Only Levites were to move the ark and they were to carry it with poles on their shoulders. Even under those circumstances if the Levites touched the ark it was at the cost of their lives (Numbers 4:15).

On the way to Jerusalem the oxen stumbled and the ark began to fall. Uzzah, the driver of the cart, placed his hand against the ark to save it from falling. But when he did, he was struck dead.

Psalms

After the ark was finally brought into Jerusalem, David declared a celebration of thanksgiving. He appointed Levites to carry the ark and conduct services. David wrote a psalm of thanksgiving, one of the most beautiful psalms found in the Old Testament (1 Chronicles 16), to be sung by Asaph. David's heart broke forth in those magnificent words, "Great is the Lord and most worthy of praise." The people were to remember the covenant that God had made with Abraham. They were to sing that the whole world should praise Him as the only living God.

The climax of the psalm is praise to God, as the source of their salvation.

As David approached the end of his reign over Israel, he again offered gratitude to the Lord, in a beautiful psalm found in 2 Samuel 22—23. The introduction (vs. 3-4) is the basis for all the many expressions of praise that follow: "The Lord is my rock, my fortress and my deliverer."

The Lord had delivered David from the bond of his enemies, even from King Saul in earlier days. When David fled from his enemies he hid in the rocky hills of Judea. As these rocks protected him from his physical enemies, so God was his eternal spiritual protector. When bound by the cords of death, the Lord heard his cry and answered. Like a thunderbolt from Heaven the Lord came down to lift him out of trouble. The Lord repaid David according to his righteousness. David walked in the light of the God of his salvation.

David's attitude reflected a principle of true spirituality, one of heartfelt gratitude. If we are grateful for what the Lord has done for us, we will express that gratitude through a life of faithful obedience.

week 16

Monday ☐ 2 Samuel 13—16
Tuesday ☐ 2 Samuel 17—19
Psalms 3, 63
Psalms 41, 55
Wednesday ☐ 2 Samuel 20, 21, 23:8—24:25
1 Chronicles 20, 21
Thursday ☐ 1 Kings 1
1 Chronicles 22—25
Psalms 2, 4—6
Friday ☐ Psalms 7—9, 11—14, 16, 17, 19—23

Look for:
- Brother murders brother
- Hanging between heaven and earth
- A kiss from Joab
- Crowned at Gihon

David was a man after God's own heart, but even he had days that were dark with sin. He had an illicit affair with Uriah's wife and tried to cover it by ordering the murder of Uriah. Bathsheba gave birth to David's son, but as a punishment the child was taken in death. The death of the child was a harbinger of the distress that was to befall David in the days to come.

David had a beautiful daughter named Tamar. Amnon, David's son and her half-brother, was filled with lust for her. With the devious help of Jonadab he forced his half-sister to commit sin with him. When Absalom, Tamar's brother, heard of it he murdered Amnon. Absalom had to flee for his life and spent three years in exile.

Rebellion

Joab influenced David to let Absalom return to Jerusalem, but David's generosity worked against him. Before long Absalom raised a conspiracy against David—and, strange to say, the people of Israel deserted David and began to follow Absalom. David had to leave Jerusalem and run for his life. The glorious king was degraded to the lowly position of a fugitive!

Absalom led the army of Israel in pursuit of David. The faithful few, under the command of Joab, defeated Israel, and the slaughter that day was 20,000 men. David instructed Joab to deal gently with his son Absalom, but Joab and his soldiers killed him. When David received the news, his terrible heartbreak was expressed in the pathetic words, "O my son Absalom! O Absalom, my son, my son!" (2 Samuel 19:4)

David committed adultery and tried to hide it with murder. As a result his home was shattered by sexual sin among his children, hatred, the murder of one son by another, Absalom rebelling and attempting to seize the throne, and finally the death of Absalom. We may view David's life as one of kingly glory, but David paid the price for willful sin.

The Succession

Though it was common knowledge in David's household that his son Solomon was to be the next king, another son, Adonijah, contrived to take over the throne. Not once did David ever displease Adonijah by saying, "Why have you done thus and so?" (1 Kings 1:6) David's indulgence of his son was now bearing fruit.

Adonijah gathered a following and proclaimed himself king of Israel. His select group was shouting, "Long live King Adonijah." Nathan, the prophet, immediately went to Bathsheba, informed her of the move of Adonijah, and suggested that she remind David that Solomon was to be the next king.

David instructed Nathan and

Zadok, the priest, to take Solomon to Gihon and anoint him king of Israel. The response of the people was, "Long live King Solomon." The intrigue of Adonijah came to a quick and sudden end.

When the death of David was near he called Solomon into his presence for his final instructions. He told Solomon, "I am about to go the way

of all the earth. So be strong, show yourself a man, and observe what the Lord your God requires" (1 Kings 2:2, 3). What better advice could a father give to his son? Much modern philosophy to the contrary, the godly life is the manly life. David was a poet, musician, and warrior but above all, in spite of failures along the way, he was a great man of God.

week 17

Monday ☐ Psalms 25—32, 35—40
Tuesday ☐ Psalms 53, 58, 61, 62, 64, 65, 68—70, 86, 101
Wednesday ☐ Psalms 103, 109, 110, 122, 124, 131, 133, 138—141, 143—145
Thursday ☐ Psalms 42—44, 49, 84, 85, 87, 88
Psalms 50, 73, 75—77
Friday ☐ Psalms 78, 80—83, 89

Look for:
- "In the great assembly I will praise the Lord" (26)
- For those who say, "Aha, aha" (70)
- The order of Melchizedek (110)
- "O Shepherd of Israel" (80)

"Shout aloud and sing for joy,
      people of Zion,
for great is the Holy One
      of Israel among you"
(Isaiah 12:6)

Psalms has been called the hymnbook of Israel (many of the psalms have instructions to the musicians as to how to accompany the singing of the psalms). Friendship with the Lord will put a song in your heart.

Both the content and the style of the psalms of Israel have an enthralling beauty. The words, "The Lord is my light and my salvation; whom shall I fear?" (Psalm 27:1) have a content that sounds the depths of the soul.

The Hebrew writers had a lyrical style that is different from English poetry. English poetry is characterized by meter and rhyme; the characteristic of Hebrew poetry is parallelism—two lines saying the same thought.

Man is emotional as well as intellectual. The psalms present a true devotional experience to be enjoyed because they appeal to both of these human traits. Psalms is primarily a guide for the devotional needs of individual followers of the Lord. By meditating upon them, an individual can learn to lift acceptable praise to the Lord.

Psalm 25, a Psalm of David

In this psalm, David is praying to the Lord for protection and guidance. Note how David sets forth God's character as he lifts his prayer. God is addressed as One who is merciful and gracious. He has steadfast love and goodness. He is faithful to the word of His covenant. Many theologians present the God of the Old Testament as vindictive, vengeful, and arbitrary, and the God of the New Testament as a God of love. God fully revealed His love in the New Testament, but how can we read David's prayer without concluding that he reveled in God's love and grace? He appeals for forgiveness of his sins on the basis of God's love and mercy.

David also petitions for guidance. One of the great expressions of God's love is His revelation of the manner of life we should live to be acceptable to Him. God not only provides forgiveness, but He instructs the faithful in the way they should go. Those that fear the Lord will enjoy the friendship of the Lord.

Petition, forgiveness, and guidance are evident in the life of the Lord's faithful people.

Psalm 40, a Psalm of David

This is a psalm of thanksgiving and personal submission to the will of God. David reminisces on God's concern for him. He says he could not number God's wondrous deeds. Many times we let our minds stay on the problems of life and forget all of God's expressions of love toward us. David had his dark experiences and so do we. With faith even during these experiences we can still offer thanksgiving to God for all His wondrous deeds.

Psalm 110, the Psalm of the Priest-King

There are more quotations in the New Testament from this psalm than from any other. It is one of the most highly Messianic psalms of all. It is quoted by Christ, by Peter on Pentecost, and by the writer of Hebrews.

In a dispute with the Pharisees, Christ cites this psalm to expose their false concepts of the Messiah (Matthew 22:41-46). His inference is that if they had accepted Him as the Christ, they would have known the meaning of the Psalm. Peter quotes the psalm to prove that it was not David but the Christ who ascended to Heaven to sit at the right hand of God (Acts 2:34, 35). The writer of Hebrews quotes it to show that the Levitical priesthood was to be replaced by the priesthood of Christ (Hebrews 7:17).

This psalm shouts to the world that Jesus is the Christ, the Son of God.

week 18

Monday ☐ Psalms 1, 10, 33, 66, 67, 71, 91—95, 97—99
Tuesday ☐ Psalms 100, 102, 104, 107, 111—117
Wednesday ☐ Psalms 118, 119
Thursday ☐ Psalms 120, 121, 123, 125, 126, 128—130, 132, 134, 146—150
Friday ☐ 1 Chronicles 26—29
2 Samuel 23:1-7
1 Kings 2:1-12

Look for:

- The evils of conceit (10)
- "Shout for joy to the Lord, all the earth" (100)
- "His love endures forever" (118)
- The words of a true father

Psalm 1, the Two Ways of Life

Psalm 1 is looked upon by many as the prologue to the entire book. It captures the whole thrust of the remainder of the psalms. Walk in the way of the Lord and be blessed or walk in the way of the wicked and perish.

The psalm teaches the intensity with which we should walk in God's way. It is one thing to occasionally give thought to God's Word, and another to keep His Word in mind day and night. A life that is constantly centered on God's Word is fruitful and full.

Psalm 104, Exaltation of the God of Creation

Today, materialistic science rules out God. All the complexities of biological life are the result of random variation. But the psalmist bows before God as the creator of the world. Natural law is a display of the wisdom of God. It is under His control and it is His means of sustaining life on earth.

The psalmist exalts God for His glory, majesty, and omnipotence. God uplifted the mountains and set bounds for the seas. He gave life-giving waters; He provided food for all life, including man. The psalmist summarizes his praise by saying, "In wisdom you made them all; the earth is full of your creatures" (v. 24).

Psalm 111, a Psalm in Praise of God

Psalms 111, 112, and 113 are the Hallelujah Psalms; they each begin with "Praise the Lord." The Lord is to be praised for who He is and what He has done for His people. This and the 112th psalm are also known as the Alphabet Psalms; each has 22 lines that begin, in order, with the 22 letters of the Hebrew alphabet. This series of acrostic lines is a trait of Hebrew poetry.

The psalmist associates gratitude and remembrance; when reviewing all that God has done, the response of the good heart is thanksgiving. God has also given us His precepts—His Word, which makes possible our redemption.

"The fear of the Lord is the beginning of wisdom," he concludes. Remembrance produces gratitude, and the end result is awesome respect for the Lord.

Psalm 117,
God's Invitation
to the Gentiles

This is the shortest of all the psalms, but it contains the most tremendous message in the world. This psalm looks forward to the day when all peoples will praise the Lord. (In Romans 15:7-12, Paul quotes this psalm and applies it to the work of Christ.) How grateful we ought to be for this little psalm with the great message!

Psalm 130,
Out of the Depths

The heart of man is overwhelmed when his sin-guilt crushes him to the ground. All of us have shared this experience with the writer of this psalm. Out of the depths of sin come our cries, and God hears and forgives. "With the Lord there is unfailing love," and He engulfs us with His redemption.

What other song could thrill the heart as greatly as this? Therefore, the psalmist says, "O Israel, put your hope in the Lord!"

week 19

Monday ☐ 1 Kings 2:13—4:34
           2 Chronicles 1:1-13
           Psalm 72
           Psalm 45
Tuesday ☐ 1 Kings 5, 6
           2 Chronicles 2:1—5:1
Wednesday ☐ 1 Kings 7:13—8:66
Thursday ☐ 1 Kings 7:1-12
           2 Chronicles 5:2—8:18
           Psalms 135, 136
Friday ☐   2 Chronicles 1:14-17;
           9:1-31
           1 Kings 9—11

Look for:
- Prayers for the king
- Building the temple
- Social changes in Israel
- The seeds of Solomon's demise
- God's blessings on His servants
- Wisdom and foolishness

Kings and Chronicles

The books of Kings and Chronicles are not primarily histories (in our sense of the word) of the kingdoms of Israel and Judah. They are theological narratives that highlight selected events, events chosen for their significance in demonstrating the ongoing relationship between Israel and her God. Every king is mentioned, but only a few are given more than a paragraph or two. Political importance has little to do with selection. Those that are singled out are the especially wicked or the notably righteous.

There are many informative parallels between the book of Deuteronomy and the books of Kings. The history of Israel is assessed from the perspective of Deuteronomy. This should not surprise us, but it often goes unnoticed.

Solomon and His Kingdom

The text does not give a great number of details about Solomon's political activity, but we have enough to know that profound changes took place within Israel. Think about the consequences for the average Israelite of Solomon's forced labor policy, his court's food requirements, his division of the nation into twelve districts (which did

42

not adhere to old tribal lines), the ceding of land to Tyre, and the expensive building projects (temple, palace complex, and administrative and military cities).

Solomon's prayer for wisdom assured his place in Israel's history, for God generously answered that request. Wisdom in the Old Testament has a very practical emphasis—the skillful application of knowledge to daily life. The ancient Near East in Solomon's day (and before) was full of wise men and seekers of wisdom. Egyptian and Mesopotamian sages have left us their writings. Solomon surpassed them all. One is always amazed how Solomon the wise man, the temple builder, the king of God's choosing, could also become Solomon the despot and apostate. Wisdom, wealth, and wives were a potent combination that Solomon could not handle.

The Temple

The amount of space devoted to the details of the temple show us the main interest of the section on Solomon. The building of the temple is the highlight of Solomon's reign. It became the place that God chose for Israel to worship Him (see Deuteronomy 12). Picture the temple's size. It was no more than a small chapel, and would have been vastly overshadowed by Solomon's royal buildings (1 Kings 7:1-12).

Psalms

Psalms 72 and 45 celebrate the blessings that God bestows on His chosen king. They serve to highlight the tragedy of Solomon. On the other hand one can imagine Psalms 135 and 136 as great hymns of Israel as the people stood before the temple proclaiming in song all that God had done for them.

week

20

Monday ☐ Song of Solomon 1—8
Tuesday ☐ Psalm 127
Proverbs 1—5
Wednesday ☐ Proverbs 6—10
Thursday ☐ Proverbs 11—15
Friday ☐ Proverbs 16—21

Look for:

- Metaphors for physical beauty
- 13 lessons for the young man
- The arduous path to wisdom
- The proverb that speaks directly to you

Song of Solomon

The Song of Solomon, or better, the Song of Songs, is one of the most unusual books in the Old Testament. At various times its emphasis on love and physical beauty has embarrassed interpreters. Consequently, the Song has often been interpreted in a nonliteral way. Many have seen it as an allegory of the love between God and Israel (the Jews) or between Christ and the church (Christians). In fact, one Christian writer, Bernard of Clairvaux (11th century A.D.), was able to preach 86 allegorical sermons on the first two chapters alone!

The book is a series of love poems that praise the devotion between a maiden and her lover. Taken literally, the book is a censure on lust, polygamy, and infidelity. It encourages love that is exclusive and absorbing and unquenchable. It endorses physical love as being a part of a legitimate relationship.

The Song's inclusion in the Bible demonstrates that the Bible has a view of the wholeness of the human being. God did create man and woman for each other (Genesis 2), and physical love is a part of that. Within an exclusive and legitimate relationship, it is to be celebrated and enjoyed. At times the church and Christians have had difficulty maintaining this wholesome view.

Proverbs

The book of Proverbs, though attributed to Solomon, has material that is not from him. It has become a repository for material from varied sources—the wise in 22:17ff; Agur in chapter 30; Lemuel in 31:1-9. Solomon's proverbs are found in 10:1—22:16 and 25:1—29:27. The latter proverbs were collected by scribes of king Hezekiah near the close of the eighth century.

Wisdom was understood in ancient Israel to be the attainment of skillful use of knowledge or talents. Chapter 1:2-7 makes it quite clear that the foundation for wisdom is theological—it is grounded in the fear of God. In one sense the book of Proverbs is the most "practical" of Bible books, but that does not mean that the other books are impractical.

The reader will notice a difference in style between chapters 1—9 and 10ff. In chapters 1—9 one finds extended essays of instructions to the young man. There are numerous addresses to "my son" and repeated warnings to avoid wicked men and loose women. The true proverb is found in the later chapters. The style of these proverbs is that of short, pithy saying, usually with two lines, the second line being in parallel with the first, or more likely in contrast with the first. There are a few extended sayings that cover more than one verse.

Generally there is little relationship between the verses. Thus, it is difficult to read several chapters of Proverbs at one sitting. Rather each verse is intended to be read and savored, reflected on and absorbed, so that it becomes a guide for daily living.

week 21

Monday ☐ Proverbs 22—26
Tuesday ☐ Proverbs 27—31
Wednesday ☐ Ecclesiastes 1—6
Thursday ☐ Ecclesiastes 7—12
Friday ☐ 1 Kings 12:1—14:20
2 Chronicles 10:1—11:4

Look for:

- The ideal woman
- Hints of faith; parallels to modern culture (in Ecclesiastes)
- Jeroboam's condemnation
- The division of Israel

More Proverbs

The remaining chapters in Proverbs include varied material. Chapter 22:17—23:22, "The Sayings of the Wise" is unusual. Since 1923 when an Egyptian scholar published an ancient Egyptian document called "Teaching of Amenemope" it has been recognized that there are many parallels in the verses in Proverbs with the Egyptian material. With the universal concern for wisdom in that period, it should not surprise us that Proverbs shares some insights with non-Israelites. Note how the introduction to these verses calls for alert attention to the teaching and concentration on the content, which will lead to trust in God and the ability to answer correctly those who depend on the learner. The teachers of wisdom were not interested in relaying pious platitudes, but in providing for a way of life.

There is an excellent way to mine the riches of Proverbs if one is willing to invest some time. Obtain a good Bible concordance, such as Young's or Strong's, identify some key words in Proverbs, and then collect all the verses that mention that word. With some effort one can produce a topical index to the book that will pay delightful dividends.

Ecclesiastes

Ecclesiastes is considered one of the strangest books in the Old Testament. Its pessimism and apparent fatalism seem out of step with the rest of the teaching of the Bible.

One of the most attractive interpretations of the book sees it as an apologetic work. This view suggests that the author is addressing the world, meeting it on its own ground, and convicting it of the inherent meaninglessness (vanity) in everything. The book is, therefore, a critique of secularism and secularized religion, of a materialism that reduces all of life to worldly pursuit.

Though the tone of the book is negative, the author should not be thought of as a skeptic. Rather, his statement that all is vanity is not his verdict on life in general, but upon the point of view that treats the world as an end in itself. He can be a destructive critic only because he knows that there is a positive value. But he keeps this in the background because his immediate aim is to dispel all false and illusory hopes that possess the secular man. His point is that when man makes the world an end in itself and makes his chief aim to gain the world, then everything turns to vanity. By denying all

human possibilities he clears the way for God!

The End of Solomon

Despite Solomon's great reputation and wisdom his reign ended in shambles. The seeds of discontent sown during his reign made it impossible for his son to keep the kingdom together. The nation became two: Israel (north) and Judah (south). Civil war ensued and the split became permanent. Perhaps the worst tragedy was that the new king in the north, Jeroboam, became a standard of wickedness for all the northern kings.

week

22

Monday ☐ 1 Kings 14:21—15:24
2 Chronicles 11:5—16:14
Tuesday ☐ 1 Kings 15:25—19:21
Wednesday ☐ 1 Kings 20:1—22:40
Thursday ☐ 2 Chronicles 17—20
1 Kings 22:41-53
2 Kings 1
Friday ☐ 2 Kings 2:1—8:15

Look for:

• References to Jeroboam
• The changing relationship between Israel and Judah
• Evaluation of the prophets
• Parallels between Elisha and Christ

Israel Divided

The consequences of the division of the nation are spelled out in the chapters for reading this week. Almost overnight Israel went from the strongest nation in the ancient Near East to two small, bickering states. The financial consequences of the collapse of the empire were catastrophic; never again was Israel dominant in the area. Though Israel as a nation (or as two) existed for several hundred years, its heyday as a powerful state lasted less than two generations!

The religious innovations initiated by Jeroboam in the north earned him condemnation. Notice how often the author seizes the opportunity to refer to Jeroboam's sin. The northern kings are all evaluated in terms of whether or not they continued in his ways. Although some of these chapters can be tedious reading, it is important to follow the intention of the author—he is tracing out the continued apostasy of Israel that eventually leads to her downfall.

Important events were happening elsewhere in the ancient Near East at this time as well. Two countries were expanding their influence—Syria (Damascus) and Assyria. Syria

was the immediate threat to Israel, especially during the later years of Elijah and Elisha's time. But Assyria was the long-range threat, inexorably becoming the dominant world power.

Prophets

Although prophets were not new in Israel, in these chapters in 1 and 2 Kings they played a very important role. The space given to Elijah, Micaiah, and Elisha tells us that they were vital to Israel's well-being.

The prophets were God's messengers to the king and the people. They first appeared in 1 Samuel, after the people insisted on a king. It was the prophet's function to preserve God's Word for the people, because the office of the king became not an avenue to God, but a path to apostasy.

In these chapters in Kings, Elijah appears to save Israel. Ahab, the son of the powerful Omri, and his wife instituted measures that would have ultimately led to the snuffing out of true covenantal faith. Elijah did nothing less than save the nation for God! It is a crucial moment. Elisha continued that ministry.

The careers of these two included a very unusual element, as far as the Old Testament is concerned: the appearance of the miraculous. Other prophets didn't minister in this way; why should these two? Perhaps it was because true faith was at such a low ebb that it took the unusual to capture the people's attention and turn them back to God.

The brief appearance of Micaiah is full of interesting details and offers us some insights into the Biblical view of God's sovereignty over every event.

week

23

Monday □ Joel 1—3
2 Kings 8:16-29
2 Chronicles 21:1-20
Tuesday □ 2 Kings 9—11
2 Chronicles 22, 23
Wednesday □ 2 Kings 12, 13
2 Chronicles 24
Thursday □ 2 Kings 14—17
Friday □ 2 Chronicles 25—28

Look for:

- The day of the Lord
- Why kings are judged
  good or bad
- Political successes and failures
- Similarities between 2 Kings 17
  and Deuteronomy

Joel

Unlike other prophetic books, Joel gives no date for itself. For that reason, it is difficult to tie him into any specific historical period. Joel is noted for three themes: the introduction of an "apocalyptic" tone, that is, projecting historical events on a cosmic scale and using vivid symbols, like the locust plague, as symbols of judgment; the day of the Lord concept; and the future outpouring of the Spirit. We also find other typical prophetic concerns: judgment on Israel's sins, hope if Israel repents, judgment on other nations, the restoration of Zion.

Note these themes both in Joel and the other prophets.

The Fortunes of Israel

The time covered in these chapters this week is over a century (849-722 B.C.), but it doesn't take much space. There are two important times in Israel's history from this period—the revolt of Jehu and the reign of Jeroboam II.

Jehu's revolt fulfilled Elijah's prophecy concerning the dynasty of Ahab—it was completely wiped out (2 Kings 9:25, 26, 36). Religiously, the revolt was important; politically, it was a disaster. Jehu effectively destroyed the existing government leading to a 50-year period of weakness, which was reversed finally by Jeroboam II.

Jeroboam's reign happily coincided with a period of weakness in both Syria and Assyria, and he was able to lead in expansion and prosperity in Israel. There are, however, only a few hints of this in Kings. The book of Amos details some of the wealth accumulated by the upper classes during Jeroboam's 41 years. The fleeting importance of affluence is amply demonstrated by the fact that within 25 years of Jeroboam's death, Israel fell to the Assyrians. Internal spiritual rot, grossly ineffective leadership, and Assyrian resurgence all contributed to that fall.

Judah

Judah's fortunes were less mercurial than Israel's during this period. They always maintained a descendant of David on the throne and several of the kings were good kings, doing what was right before God (Asa, Jehoshaphat, Uzziah/Amaziah, and later Hezekiah and Josiah). The only aberration was when Athaliah, the queen-mother and daughter of Ahab, seized the throne at the death of her son. But in a few years she was

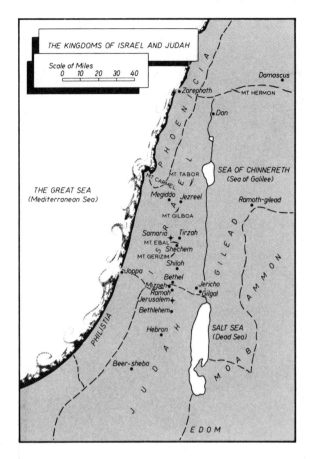

killed by priests who put her grandson and rightful heir on the throne.

The Fall

The fall of Samaria to Assyria occurred in 722/21 B.C. It was the end of the northern kingdom. The Assyrians would exile the leaders of captured nations among other nations and bring in foreigners to repopulate the newly captured country. This policy effectively ended Israel's national identity.

The book of Kings includes a long essay on the reasons for Israel's fall: apostasy and idolatry. Even God's longsuffering could not overcome the people's persistence in sin.

week 24

Monday ☐ Jonah 1—4
           Hosea 1—4
Tuesday ☐ Hosea 5—14
Wednesday ☐ Amos 1—9
Thursday ☐ Micah 1—7
Friday ☐ Isaiah 6
          Isaiah 1—5

Look for:
- Style of prophetic writings
- A prayer from the bottom of the sea
- God's "wife," Israel
- Isaiah before the throne of God

Prophetic Literature

Some of the richest reading in the Old Testament is in store this week. These prophets are among the best loved and most studied in the Old Testament. They are to be savored and digested slowly.

Most of the prophetic literature is in poetry, so we must read the prophets with a great deal of sensitivity to the language and style. Hebrew poetry is characterized by parallelism of thought, not rhyme. A thought stated in one line may be repeated in different words in the next line (Hosea 2:6), or expanded (2:8), or contrasted (11:3). Sometimes the parallelism of thought will extend for three or four lines. Hebrew poetry is also noted for its figures of speech (metaphors, similes, exaggerations), local color, and veiled references to history and culture. Therefore, we must read the prophets carefully to catch their depth of meaning.

It is important to recognize that the prophetic books are collections of sermons; often a chapter contains more than one unit of thought.

Jonah

This book is more than just a well-known children's story. It is the only book of prophecy that is mostly narrative, and its theme is God's mercy to a disobedient world (God's own people included). Christ would later refer to His own burial in the earth as "the sign of Jonah," saying that this would be the only sign given to the wicked generation that kept seeking miracles as proof that Jesus was sent from God.

Hosea

Hosea is best known for developing the marriage imagery that became such a powerful metaphor for describing the relationship between God and His people. The imagery is especially vivid in Hosea's sermons because of the Canaanite religion he was combating. The Israelites had apostasized to the Canaanite fertility religion, with its sacred prostitution and its myths of sexually active gods. Hosea's use of the marriage imagery in a sense beards the lion in its own den. Chapter 2 especially details how he turns the marriage imagery to his advantage.

Hosea has also some of the most tender expressions of God's love for Israel (chapter 11) and a powerful statement on repentance (chapter 14). His sermons went unheeded and the northern kingdom fell soon after his preaching (perhaps even in his own lifetime).

Amos

Amos gives us a glimpse into the social conditions within Israel during the reign of the powerful Jeroboam II (2 Kings 14:23-29). It was a time of prosperity but also oppression, and Amos' concern for the poor is well known. Amos also has a profound understanding of the universal sovereignty of God. In chapters 1 and 2 he makes it clear that all nations must be accountable to Him. Amos and Hosea are the only two prophets who speak to the northern kingdom. All other writing prophets preach to Judah or foreign nations.

Micah

Micah is a contemporary of Isaiah and shares the concerns of both Amos and Isaiah.

Isaiah

Isaiah is one of the best known prophets. It is important to note chapter 6 in its entirety. Isaiah was called to failure! His very preaching would be the cause of resistance among the stubborn people. Chapter 1 contains a summary of most of the preaching points Isaiah makes in the rest of the book.

week 25

Monday ☐ Isaiah 7—13
Tuesday ☐ Isaiah 14—22
Wednesday ☐ Isaiah 23—28
Thursday ☐ Isaiah 29—35
Friday ☐ Isaiah 36—39

Look for:
- Promises of a coming King
- Sins of the nations
- Isaiah's view of the future
- God's holiness
- Assyria threatens Judah
- New Testament use of Isaiah

Isaiah's Structure

In a long book like Isaiah, it is important to note the structure for help in putting the material together as it is read. Chapters 1—6 serve as an introduction and background and probably come from Isaiah's earliest time (the first years after 740 B.C.). Chapters 7—12 occur during the reign of Ahaz and offer hope under Assyrian oppression through a connected series of promises centering on sons to be born. Chapters 13—23 are strictures against other nations. Chapters 24—27 speak of judgment of the world and last things. Chapters 28—39 come from the time of Hezekiah and offer words of judgment and hope. A recurring theme throughout the whole of Isaiah is that God is "the Holy One of Israel."

The Sons and the Nations

It is important to note the emphasis on sons in chapters 7—12.

Chapter 7 is well-known but not often read in its context by Christians. It must be remembered as first of all a message to Ahaz's unbelief. The prophet's own son is in view in chapter 8. In fact, both of Isaiah's sons were walking sermons (note the meanings of their names!) The divine prince of chapter 9 is also well-known to Christians, but try reading it from the perspective of one of Isaiah's contemporaries, in a time of evil kings and a weak state. The shoot from the stump of Jesse in chapter 11 is especially endowed with the spirit. Compare his endowment with the benefits of wisdom in Proverbs 1.

The God of Israel is the sovereign Lord; every nation is accountable to Him. The nations were judged by how they lived up to their own international contracts and by how they treated God's people. God's sovereignty over the nations has not changed since Old Testament times.

God's Judgment

In chapters 24—27, Isaiah is concerned not with the present, but with God's final victory over evil and His universal judgment. Yet, this is still a message for the people of his day, for it means the final salvation for God's people. Man has brought chaos to the world, but God's judgment will lead to a new age of security and peace.

Hezekiah

The last chapters in this section come from the time of Hezekiah. This was an especially threatening time, as chapters 36—39 make clear. Hezekiah was a good king. His trust in God in the face of overwhelming

odds brought deliverance to Jerusalem and Judah. This victory of faith was remembered a long time in Judah, though the fact that it was based on faith was soon forgotten. God's promises for the safety and security of Zion (Jerusalem) were soon taken as unconditional promises by God, and it was forgotten that Hezekiah had first repented of sin. Jeremiah's later struggle with this entrenched dogmatic article of faith nearly cost him his life (Jeremiah 7 and 26).

week 26

Monday ☐ 2 Kings 18—20
　　　　　　Psalms 46—48
Tuesday ☐ 2 Chronicles 29—32
Wednesday ☐ Isaiah 40—43
Thursday ☐ Isaiah 44—48
Friday ☐ Isaiah 49—54

Look for:
- Hezekiah's character
- Celebrations of God as king
- God's deliverance from captivity
- Hymns of praise and thanksgiving
- The role of the servant

Two Views of a Good King

The different emphases of Kings and Chronicles are apparent in this week's reading. Both agree that Hezekiah was a good king, but Kings is interested in how his faithfulness saved Jerusalem and Chronicles is interested in the details of his religious reform. Psalms 46—48 celebrate the reign and rule of God, the true, great king. What glorious joy that His faithful representative should be reigning over Judah!

Isaiah

Even the casual reader will note a break in style and subject matter between Isaiah 39 and 40. Chapters 1—39 are mostly coming judgment on Judah. Beginning with chapter 40 the emphasis is on deliverance from captivity in Babylon. In fact, chapters 38 and 39 prepare for the later chapters by looking ahead to the coming power of Babylon. We have a new beginning in chapter 40, with an emphasis on the good news to be preached. The descriptions in the following chapters of God bringing his people back to the land are some of the most beautiful passages in the Old Testament.

The differences in style have been variously explained. One reason certainly is the different subject matter, for now it is the task of the prophet to proclaim hope to the captives and the glorious message of return. Since the prophecies concern a return from captivity, many have denied that Isaiah could have written these chapters, for the captivity occurred over a century after Isaiah's time. However, one is led to such an extreme position only if one first denies Isaiah's capacity, under God's inspiration, to take a long look into the future.

These chapters would also be a message of great comfort to the faithful during the dark days of Manasseh that followed Hezekiah's reign. The important theme that God is "the Holy One of Israel" continues in these chapters.

God and the gods

In those days it was universally believed that a god and the fortunes of his people were inextricably bound together. If a nation was conquered by another, that meant that the god of the conquered nation was impotent, and would fade away. A majority in Israel probably shared this view, and the captivity would have been a great shock. That is why these chapters have such an emphasis on God's sovereign power (40:12-31).

The Servant Songs

Four passages in Isaiah have been isolated as relating to each other in theme—God will raise up a "servant" to carry out His work (42:1-4; 49:1-6; 50:4-9; 52:13—53:12). This servant is empowered with the spirit of God, yet goes about his work quietly in face of great opposition. The only adequate identification of the servant is that of the Messiah. The last song contains the most perfect picture in Scripture of the Messiah's atoning work.

week 27

Monday ☐ Isaiah 55—60
Tuesday ☐ Isaiah 61—66
Wednesday ☐ 2 Kings 21
2 Chronicles 33
Obadiah
Thursday ☐ 2 Kings 22, 23
Zephaniah 1—3
Friday ☐ 2 Chronicles 34, 35
Nahum 1—3

Look for:
- Sham religion
- God's people come home
- The "new" in the future
- Compare Josiah to Hezekiah
- Judah's sins, according to Zephaniah

New Things in the Future

The reader will find in Isaiah's last chapters a rather loose structure, in contrast to the obvious structure in the earlier chapters. We find here material about Judah before and after the exile and about the distant future of Israel. It is difficult to read with understanding, yet there are magnificent themes here. There are strictures against sham religion (chapters 58, 59), a vision of Zion's glorious future (60—62), God's vengeance on the nations (63:1-7), and a new heaven and earth (65). It is interesting that Isaiah should end on the note that it does in 66:22-24. It reminds us that man's continuous rebellion against God makes it necessary for the ministry of His suffering servant.

Judah's Worst and Best Kings

It seems incredible that a good king like Hezekiah could have a son like Manasseh. Manasseh's reign was marked by full-scale overturning of all of Hezekiah's reforms and the introduction of not one, but several pagan religions. It was further marked by severe persecutions of the faithful. The "innocent blood" of 2 Kings 21:16 probably means Judeans loyal to God. The situation was intensified by the fact that Manasseh's reign was so long (55 years), though this included several years as co-regent with Hezekiah.

It also seems amazing that such a good king as Josiah could have followed Manasseh (after Amon's brief reign). With Hezekiah, Josiah was the best king Judah had. His religious reform even exceeded Hezekiah's. Josiah had the good fortune of being king at a time when Assyria was crumbling and Babylon was not yet at its zenith. This left a power vacuum in the Middle East, which allowed Josiah to initiate a time of independence, expansion, and prosperity for Judah. It must have seemed like a new and glorious era to those faithful who had survived the days of Manasseh. Even the average Judean had high hopes for the future. Therefore, Josiah's tragic death in battle must have shattered many dreams.

That Judah fell to Babylon within 22 years of his death is testimony to the ineptness and continued hard-headed rebellion against God by the leadership in Judah.

Zephaniah

Probably Zephaniah was the first to break the long prophetic silence after Manasseh's reign. We find here some details of the pagan religions and the typical prophetic themes: God's judgment on Jerusalem, on the nations, and the ultimate redemption of God's people with God dwelling in their midst.

Nahum

Nahum exults as he sees the coming fall of Nineveh, the capital of Assyria. This, of course, would signal the collapse of Assyria, that evil nation to which Judah had been in bondage for so long. Nineveh fell in 612 B.C. Isaiah had long before seen this as judgment on its arrogance (Isaiah 10).

week

28

Monday ☐ Habakkuk 1—3
Jeremiah 1, 11, 12
Tuesday ☐ Jeremiah 2—5
Wednesday ☐ 2 Kings 23:31—24:20
2 Chronicles 36:1-16
Daniel 1
Jeremiah 6
Thursday ☐ Jeremiah 7—10
Friday ☐ Jeremiah 18—20, 25, 26

Look for:
- "I am going to do something you would not believe"
- Living by faith in God
- God speaks to Jeremiah
- Stop believing you are safe

"Why, God?"

The last years of Judah witnessed the ministries of several important prophets. One of the lesser known is Habakkuk. His date is not certain, but he probably preached between 626 and 609 B.C. His book is not a record of his sermons but a dialogue between himself and God. His questions are modern ones: "Why? Why don't you do something, God?" Then when God does, "Why did you do it that way?" God's answer is not so much to the question but to Habakkuk—the righteous will live by faithfulness!

Jeremiah

One of the best known prophets of this period is Jeremiah. He began preaching during the reign of Josiah and continued on through the fall of Jerusalem in 587. We know more about Jeremiah than any other prophet because the book contains several biographical chapters, probably written by Baruch. Jeremiah is known for his close encounters with death and for his complaints against God. He is also one of the few prophets who predicted the fall of Jerusalem and lived to see it.

The chronology of the book of

Jeremiah is not straightforward, though it is generally thought the first 25 chapters are from Jeremiah's earliest preaching, ending in 597. Jeremiah 36 tells us how at least part of the book was written—Jeremiah dictated to Baruch from memory his sermons of the previous 20 years! Jeremiah is one of the best poets among the prophets, so his sermons demand close reading. We also have in Jeremiah many prose sermons. These are scattered throughout but most appear in chapters 1—25, with a few in 26—33.

A brief outline will be helpful: chapters 1—25:14 are prophecies of judgment from the time of Josiah (2—6) and Jehoiakim (7—20), and prophecies against kings and other prophets (21—25:14); chapters 26—33 are prophecies of destruction (26—29) and future restoration (30—33); chapters 34—35 are biographical, detailing Jeremiah's experiences during the last days of Jerusalem. Chapter 25:15-38 actually goes with chapters 46—51 and the prophecies against the foreign nations; chapter 52 is an historical appendix taken from 2 Kings.

The Last Years of Judah

When Josiah was killed in 609 at Megiddo, the Judeans put Jehoahaz on the throne. Three months later, the Egyptians replaced him with his brother, Jehoiakim. During Jehoiakim's reign, Babylon became the ascendant power. Jehoiakim vacillated between paying tribute and rebelling. In 598, Babylon marched against Jerusalem. Jehoiakim died during the siege and Jehoiachin, his son, succeeded him. But Jehoiachin was taken captive to Babylon along with thousands of other Judeans.

Daniel

According to Daniel 1:1, 2, the 598 deportation was the second, not the first. In 605, the Babylonians marched into Palestine and took hostages and booty from Jerusalem, Daniel among them (compare 2 Kings 24:1).

week 29

Monday ☐ Jeremiah 45—47
Jeremiah 35, 36
Tuesday ☐ Jeremiah 13—17
Wednesday ☐ Daniel 2
Jeremiah 22, 23
Thursday ☐ Ezekiel 1—7
Friday ☐ Ezekiel 8—14

Look for:
- An enormous statue
- Burning a scroll
- Jeremiah's acted sermons
- Ezekiel's personality
- References to the Spirit
- Idolatry described in Ezekiel

Jeremiah

The chapters this week include some pungent words against Judean kings and prophets. One fact not always seen clearly is that there were many prophets in Judah besides the ones we read. A few names surface (Huldah in 2 Kings 22:14 and Hananiah in Jeremiah 28), but most are nameless. Whenever Jeremiah encountered them, there was always conflict. His description in chapter 23 reflects why he opposed them. They were immoral, spoke falsehoods, pandered to the wishes of the people, and did not have an intimate relationship with God.

Daniel

Daniel is an unusual prophetic book. It doesn't fit in with the typical prophetic literature. In the Hebrew Bible, the book is included not in the prophets, but in the "Writings." It is important to have some sense of history to understand Daniel. The book covers over 60 years, from the deportation to after 539 B.C. (The Daniel who was thrown to the lions was an old man.)

Daniel has been a favorite book for study. The dreams and visions have been given a great many interpretations, most of them mutually exclusive. That should in itself warn us against any kind of dogmatism on these passages.

The main emphasis of all of Daniel is God's sovereignty over the whole world. Daniel intends to tell the cap-

tives that although they may still be in captivity, their God is in charge of the nations and is working out His will.

Ezekiel

Ezekiel was 20 years younger than Jeremiah and was one of those taken captive in 598. Like Daniel he preached to the exiles and emphasized that God was still the Lord, and would bring judgment on sin, then restore His people. He, like Jeremiah, lived through the fall of Jerusalem, but was in Babylon.

The book of Ezekiel has a straightforward style with most sections carefully dated. The sermons are mostly long prose sections. The structure is simple: chapters 1—24 are prophecies of doom on Judah and Jerusalem, with chapter 24 anticipating Jerusalem's fall; chapters 25—32 are prophecies against the nations; chapters 33—48 are sermons on the restoration of Judah and Jerusalem, with chapter 33 explaining the fall of Jerusalem.

The unusual aspect of Ezekiel is his own personality and activity. Many times he acts out his message or lives through a personal experience that ties in with the national trauma (as in chapter 34). He is also noted for his emphasis on the Spirit in his life. No other prophet claims to be empowered by the Spirit as much as Ezekiel—from the very beginning he is controlled by the Spirit. This is striking when we realize that most other prophets never mentioned the Spirit at all.

week
30

Monday ☐ Ezekiel 15—19
Tuesday ☐ Ezekiel 20—22
Wednesday ☐ Ezekiel 23
Jeremiah 48, 49
Thursday ☐ Jeremiah 24, 27—29
Jeremiah 21
Friday ☐ 2 Kings 25:1-21
2 Chronicles 36:17-21
Jeremiah 39:1-18; 52:1-30
Ezekiel 24, 25

Look for:
- Israel as a prostitute
- Ezekiel's view of
  Israel's history
- Chaos in Jerusalem
- Zedekiah: concerned for
  Jerusalem or for his own fate?

Ezekiel

The chapters for this week contain some striking sermons by Ezekiel. They were being delivered in *Babylon* just two years (and less) before the fall of Jerusalem. It was a time of anxiety among the exiles as they awaited their fate. They hoped for an early return to Judah; in fact certain prophets were telling them that (Jeremiah 29). Ezekiel's sermons seem intent on making it clear that such hopes, and indeed even hope for the survival of Jerusalem, rested on false premises. Nothing had changed and Judah's entrenched sin was terrible to behold.

One of Ezekiel's most striking extended sermon topics was based on

the marriage metaphor that Hosea first used. In chapters 16 and 23, Ezekiel develops expressive imagery of spiritual adultery, first under the allegory of a rescued foundling, then under the allegory of two unfaithful sisters. Though we may find some of the imagery and language overdone, it serves to emphasize how repulsive to God Judah's apostasy was.

The history of Judah's apostasy is laid out in chapter 20. It clearly shows the divine estimate of Israelite history and contrasts that with God acting throughout for His name's sake. A problem that Ezekiel dealt with head-on was the common complaint among the exiles that they were being punished for their father's sins. In chapter 18, Ezekiel shows the falseness of that thinking. The repeated truth rings out—"The soul who sins will die." These Judeans were no different than most people, unwilling to face up to the possibility that they might just share some of the responsibility for their plight.

The Fall of Jerusalem

Zedekiah's confusion during the last days of Jerusalem is seen in several chapters in Jeremiah. One gets the impression that Zedekiah wanted to listen to Jeremiah's counsel but did not have the fortitude to go against the wishes of his advisors. The thinking at court was that Judah should resist Babylon and hope for help from Egypt. Jeremiah said that the only way to survive was to surrender to Babylon and remain a vassal. That was treason to the court hotheads; Jeremiah was imprisoned. Zedekiah's inquiries of Jeremiah are to be understood against this background (chapters 21, 37, 38).

The fall of Jerusalem to Babylon in 587 B.C. is one of those peg dates that are to be remembered for their history-changing consequences. The people of God were never the same. The effective end of Judah/Israel as an independent people had profound psychological and spiritual consequences. From now on the prophetic message would have to be understood in the light of this event. The people had to be led to a deeper understanding of God's work in the world and be shown that God's faithfulness, and theirs, could still be maintained.

week 31

Monday ☐ Jeremiah 30, 31, 37, 38
Tuesday ☐ Jeremiah 32—34
Wednesday ☐ Ezekiel 26—31
Thursday ☐ Psalm 74
1 Chronicles 9:1
1 Chronicles 2—5
Friday ☐ 1 Chronicles 6—9

Look for:
- How Jeremiah's words "plant" Israel
- The new in the New Covenant
- The weakness of the old covenant
- The fall of the King of Tyre

Out of Judgment, Hope

Recall the account of Jeremiah's commission as a prophet in chapter 1. In verse 10 God described for Jeremiah his mission. He was appointed over nations "to uproot and tear down, to destroy and overthrow, to build and to plant."

So far in Jeremiah we have seen his uprooting and tearing down, that is, his sermons concerning God's coming judgment and destruction on apostate Judah and on pagan nations. Remember his complaint in 20:8: "Whenever I speak, I cry out proclaiming violence and destruction." This part of his mission caused him great personal distress and brought him insults. But as Jeremiah realized elsewhere, the times demanded that kind of message, and to preach anything else was to be a false prophet (23:16ff).

But now in chapters 30—33 we find Jeremiah's sermons on hope, his words of building and planting. Beyond the destruction God still had good plans for His people. He would restore Israel! These chapters emphasize an important aspect of the prophetic message, that even though God's judgment was coming on sinful Judah, there would be a restoration and the people could have hope. God's justice demanded judgment on sin, but His grace provided that a

remnant would survive and be restored. *Out of judgment* comes renewal and hope.

Although these chapters are only a fraction of the whole of Jeremiah, they contain some of the most important words of Jeremiah. What Christian can fail to realize the importance of the words on the "New Covenant" in chapter 31? The irony in this passage is that several aspects of the new covenant are not new; they were emphasized under the old covenant as well. Perhaps what Jeremiah was saying to his contemporaries was that they had traveled so far from the proper understanding of the covenant law that everything in the coming covenant would be new to them, although it shouldn't be (compare this with Ezekiel 36:26; God will give His people a new heart and new spirit!).

Ezekiel

Ezekiel's prophecies against the nations have the same general purpose as Jeremiah's. There is probably a symbolic element here—Tyre is chosen to represent godless commerce, and Egypt is chosen to represent gross idolatry. Ezekiel 28:11-19 is often interpreted as a description of the fall of Satan, but the context clearly shows it to be a description of the human pride of the king of Tyre. His end, in verses 18, 19, is portrayed as already having happened.

Geneologies

The geneological lists in 1 Chronicles were important to ancient Israel to tie the present to the past, both historically and religiously. The author here also wishes to show the importance of David and his descendants in Israel's history.

week
32

Monday ☐ 2 Kings 25:22-26
Jeremiah 40—44
Tuesday ☐ Jeremiah 50, 51
Psalm 79
Wednesday ☐ Lamentations 1—5
Thursday ☐ Ezekiel 33
Ezekiel 32, 34
Friday ☐ Ezekiel 35—39

Look for:
- Conditions in Judah after the fall
- Judah's continued idolatry
- Poetic images of grief
- Ezekiel's picture of hope
  for the future

After the Fall

The situation in Judah became grim. The Babylonians had taken the cream of the nation back to Babylon; in Judah only the lower classes and the poor were left. The cities and countryside had been devastated by the invading army. Living under these conditions was marginal—there was little food and very few ways to make a living. In a sense those taken to Babylon were better off. Judah was reduced to a totally subservient vassal to Babylon, unable even to pick her own leaders. There was still, however, resistance. The appointed governor was assassinated. The culprits fled to Egypt, taking Jeremiah with them. These were probably not the first refugees to go to Egypt.

During the last years of Judah many would have fled there for safety. This Judean colony remained in Egypt and multiplied. Though we have no more information about them in the Bible, we do know that by 300-250 B.C. they were a large group and wielded strong influence in Egypt. Out of this group came the first major, innovative request in Bible transmission—a request to have the Hebrew Bible translated into Greek. By 250, they had lost use of the Hebrew to the extent that they could no longer understand their Bible.

It is clear from Jeremiah's message to the exiles in Egypt that religiously nothing had changed. Though Jerusalem had been destroyed because of idolatry, they continued in it. In fact, some contended that the reason Jerusalem was destroyed was because they had given up idolatry (Jeremiah 44:15-18)! How amazing are the powers of rationalization, even in the face of clear preaching!

Lamentations

This book is unusual in several ways, especially in its written style. Its purpose was to express profound grief over the fall of Jerusalem. Several passages reflect eyewitness accounts of the siege.

The dirge style in Hebrew literature is unique, but it is almost impossible to render adequately in English translation. The verses are long, with three lines per verse. These lines have a special meter which, when read in Hebrew, give them a dirgelike sound. Another outstanding feature is the acrostic. There are 22 letters in the Hebrew alphabet; chapters 1, 2, and 4 have 22 verses, with the first word in each verse beginning with the succeeding Hebrew letter, from the first to the

last of the alphabet. Chapter 3 has 66 verses with the first words in each group of 3 verses sharing the same letter. This is very polished Hebrew poetry.

Grief is a part of human life and the grief over the fallen city was profound. Perhaps it can still speak to those who have suffered deep grief.

Ezekiel

The chapters in Ezekiel present his picture of God's restoration of His people. They speak of complete victory over Israel's enemies, victory won by God himself.

week 33

Monday ☐ Ezekiel 40—43
Tuesday ☐ Ezekiel 44—48
Wednesday ☐ 2 Kings 25:27-30
Jeremiah 52:31-34
Daniel 3, 4
Thursday ☐ Daniel 7, 8
Daniel 5, 11, 12
Friday ☐ Daniel 6, 9, 10
Psalm 137

Look for:

- Hints of symbolism in Ezekiel
- Symbolism in Daniel
- Daniel's faithfulness and God's power
- Interpretations of Daniel's visions

A Captive King

Jehoiachin, the king taken captive in 597, was still considered by many as the true king of Judah. Second Kings ends with a note on his good treatment at the hands of the Babylonians. Documents recovered from ancient Babylon mentioned the rations given by Nebuchadnezzar to one Ya'u-Kinu, King of Yahudu. This is undoubtedly Jehoiachin of Judah.

Apocalyptic Visions

Chapters 40—48 in Ezekiel are an extended description of Ezekiel's vision of a new, restored temple and temple worship. We have here a new form of prophecy. It is entirely visionary and symbolic. Zechariah 1—8 carries on this same style, but it is in Daniel 7—12 that this new form reaches its climax. In Daniel, the application is taken out of the prophet's own time. It is a vision of the end times in highly symbolic form with the interpretation sealed until then. This form is called "apocalyptic." The book of Revelation is the New Testament counterpart.

The interpretations of Ezekiel 40—48 suggested are varied and cannot be spelled out here. A literal interpretation seems to be the weakest. In the light of the work of

Jesus Christ in the New Testament it seems hardly credible that we should expect in the future a rebuilt temple, a renewed priesthood, and a reinstituted sacrificial system. Doesn't Hebrews show how Christ is superior in every way to all of that? It seems best to understand that there is a great deal of symbolism in these chapters. Ezekiel's purpose was to give hope to his people of a restored, organized people of God. How better to do it than in a way understandable to them? But in the fulfillment of this vision, the type and shadow loses itself in the substance, the earthly in the heavenly. Revelation 20—22 picks up on Ezekiel 38—48 in a way similar to this.

Daniel

Again, a great deal has been written about chapters 3—10 of Daniel. It must be recognized not only that this material is highly symbolic, but that also the interpretation was sealed up (8:26; 12:9). That should serve as a warning to us not to become too confident that we have fully understood. The main point, that the sovereign God is in control of the world, is clear. The details of how this sovereignty works out sometimes escapes us. That the New Testament seldom uses these chapters should also serve as a warning. Jesus uses the Son of Man language of himself, but the material in chapter 9, which is clearly Messianic, is not used.

For a clear understanding of all the readings this week, consult a good commentary, like John Taylor on Ezekiel and Joyce Baldwin on Daniel, both published by InterVarsity Press in the Tyndale Old Testament Commentary series.

week 34

Monday ☐ 2 Chronicles 36:22, 23
Ezra 1—6
Tuesday ☐ Haggai 1—3
Zechariah 1—7
Wednesday ☐ Zechariah 8—14
Thursday ☐ Esther 1—4
Friday ☐ Esther 5—10

Look for:

- Difficulties in rebuilding the temple
- Help from the Persians
- Plots to destroy the Jews
- Symbolism in Zechariah

The Jews in Babylon

We know little of what happened in Judah following the destruction of Jerusalem. Babylon left the land devastated and the population decimated. All the major cities were destroyed and not rebuilt for some time. Scholars have speculated that the population was only 20,000 compared with 250,000 just 50 years earlier.

The center of true Israel shifted to Babylon. There the exiles were allowed to establish their own towns, engage in livelihoods, and maintain their religious life. Some became quite wealthy.

World events led to a renewed vigor among the exiles. Babylon fell to Cyrus the Persian in 539. Cyrus, who by official policy acknowledged the gods of other countries, decreed that the Jews could return home. That most stayed in Babylon testifies to how little the homeland now appealed to these second generation exiles. The first order of business for the returnees was to rebuild the temple, but lack of will and outside opposition prevented it. Darius I began his long reign (36 years) in 522 and brought order to the empire. With his support, and the encouragement of Haggai and Zechariah, the temple rebuilding was finally completed in 515.

Haggai and Zechariah

Haggai preached for only three months, but he is credited with getting the temple rebuilding initiated.

He met head-on the excuses for not rebuilding, and promised material blessings from a spiritual endeavor. He also singled out Zerubbabel as an important leader.

Between Haggai's second and third messages, Zechariah began preaching. He emphasized that an inward turning to God was as necessary as an outward one.

His book divides naturally into two parts: chapters 1—8 and 9—14, with great differences between the two. Many hold that some anonymous prophet is the author of the second part. Both parts are apocalyptic, but in different ways. Chapters 1—8 contain eight visions in which Zechariah tends to blend his own time with the coming day of the Lord. God's sovereignty is stressed throughout. A favorite title for God is "The Lord Almighty" (NIV) or "The Lord of Hosts" (KJV). The symbolic nature of chapters 9—14 makes interpretation difficult. The many allusions to and quotations from these chapters in the New Testament tells us how to read them—as fulfilled in the coming of the Messiah.

Esther

This book takes us to the far eastern area of the Middle East to the Persian capital. These during the reign of Ahasuerus (*Xerxes* in Greek; 486-456), successor of Darius I, Esther came to prominence and saved her people. The Jews still celebrate that victory yearly in the feast of Purim. Though God is never mentioned by name in the book, His providential guidance is presupposed throughout.

Excavations at Shushan have confirmed many of the details of the royal complex described in Esther.

week 35

Monday ☐ Ezra 7—10
Tuesday ☐ Nehemiah 1—6
Wednesday ☐ Nehemiah 11—13
Thursday ☐ Nehemiah 7—10
Friday ☐ Malachi 1—4

Look for:

- Ezra's response to mixed marriages
- Ezra's prayer life
- Opposition to Nehemiah
- Unfaithfulness in Malachi
- Spiritual conditions in Judah

Return to Jerusalem

The books of Ezra and Nehemiah continue the history of Israel as begun in 1 and 2 Chronicles. They cover the period from the return from exile (539 B.C.) until Nehemiah's second trip to Jerusalem (after 433 B.C.). The first six chapters of Ezra deal with the return and the temple rebuilding, until 515. Then there is a large gap; Ezra 7 begins with Ezra's return in 458. In this period the population in Judah was perhaps increasing as more Jews drifted back and local conditions improved. But there was still a great deal of insecurity. In the world at large, Persia continued to control the Middle East and prosperity and peace reigned. The Jewish community in Babylon flourished and many rose to positions of prominence, Nehemiah being only one example.

Ezra's return to Judah under sponsorship of the Persian king led to at least temporary changes in Judah, for it meant that now an official appointee was there to lead. It also meant new spiritual leadership, for Ezra was a scribe and teacher of the law, there to promote adherence to the Mosaic covenant.

Nehemiah

A few years after Ezra's return, Nehemiah became concerned about the precarious position of Judah and received royal permission to go help. He arrived in 445 and with great determination rebuilt the walls of Jerusalem. During his administration, Ezra was able to lead in a great "reading of the law day," which led to national repentance and spiritual renewal. During a second term, Nehemiah had to deal with mixed marriages again.

After the time of Nehemiah we know nothing from the Bible of the Jews in Palestine until the New Testament era. Fortunately, other sources have filled in the gaps for us.

The initial spiritual problem Ezra encountered was mixed marriages. The law in Deuteronomy (7:1-5) took a firm stand against this and Ezra followed suit. This task of purifying the community took all of his energy.

Malachi

Malachi was the last of the prophets, marking the end of an era. The Jews became a people of the law, and the scribe (following Ezra) became the spiritual leader. This produced a profound change in Judaism, and the religion we meet in the New Testament is different from what we have seen in the Old Testament.

Malachi shows us the spiritual degeneration among the Judeans sometime prior to the time of Ezra. The problems are the same; they include unfaithfulness and general disrespect for God by the people and the priests. For that, judgment is again decreed.

Malachi's promise of Elijah's return figures large in Jewish Messianic expectations in the pre-New Testament times. Jesus applied Malachi's words to John the Baptist (Matthew 11:14).

The New Testament

Between the Testaments

The Old Testament ended with the restoration of the Jews to their homeland. They returned with high expectations for the Golden Age of Israel to be restored once more. But the years came and went only to be met with hardship, deprivation, and difficulty. Three significant tasks were completed—restoring the temple, rebuilding the city walls, and reestablishing the law community—but the restoration of old Israel was not to be realized.

The nearly four hundred years between the Testaments was not all peace and quiet, merely waiting for the coming of Jesus. Persia dominated Palestine until 334 B.C., when Alexander the Great of Greece conquered the known world. After his death eleven years later, his empire was divided among four generals—and Palestine was caught in the middle of a power struggle between two of them. The group that finally came to power oppressed the Jews, taxing them heavily and forbidding them to practice their religion.

In 167 B.C. the Jews rebelled, led by a group of revolutionaries called the Maccabees. Temple worship and other tenets of the Jewish religion were returned.

In 63 B.C. Palestine fell to Roman rule when Pompey led his forces against the Jews. The Herodians were appointed as puppet rulers and maintained oversight from B.C. 63—A.D. 135. The first was Antipater, whose grandson, Herod the Great, ruled from 37—4 B.C.

By the time the New Testament begins, Judaism subscribed to the centrality and authority of the Torah, or books of Law. The Jews observed the sacrificial services of the temple and believed that God's kingdom would center in Palestine. But party differences had arisen over *how* these tenets of the faith should be interpreted.

The Sadducees came from the priestly families. They claimed strict adherence to the Torah—so strict that they rejected the doctrine of the resurrection, because they found no evidence for it in the Torah. Yet they advocated a degree of compromise with the cultural surroundings, so that the temple services could continue.

On the other hand, the Pharisees, the largest and most influential group, practiced strict separatist practices: dietary rules, circumcision, fasting, prayer. They wanted nothing to do with Gentiles. Yet they accepted teachings in addition to the Torah.

The center of worship became the synagogue. Whenever ten men could be found to form a congregation, synagogues were created as a center of prayer, worship, and instruction.

It was to this world, united under Roman rule yet divided by competing philosophies, that Jesus came.

Divisions of the New Testament

Just as there are four kinds of books in the Old Testament, there are four kinds in the New Testament: Gospels, History, Letters, and Prophecy.

Gospels

The Gospels record a time of transition. They are properly listed as part of the New Testament, but in the period they cover, the Old Testament law was still in effect. They tell about the life, death, and resurrection of Jesus. Their purpose is to lead us to believe that Jesus is the Christ, the Son of God.

History

The book of history, Acts, tells how the church began, how it carried on its work, and how people became Christians. Its purpose is to show people today how to become Christians and carry on the work of the church.

Letters

The letters are addressed to Christians, but not all their teaching is intended for all Christians. There are instructions for new Christians or "babes" in Christ, and there are instructions for those who have lived in Christ and should have gone far in Christian attainment. There are instructions for deacons and elders. There are instructions for widows, parents, and children. There are instructions for servants and masters. And, of course, many parts of the letters give instructions for all who are trying to follow Christ.

Their purpose is to guide Christians in their living, helping them to do whatever Jesus commanded.

Prophecy

The book of prophecy, Revelation, tells of the final victory of Christ and His people. It is perhaps less read and less understood than any other New Testament book, because of its highly figurative language and because of the difficulty of understanding prophecies not yet fulfilled. However, the book as a whole brings a helpful and encouraging message that every Christian reader can easily grasp: Christ will have the final victory. The purpose of this book is to encourage us to keep on living as Christians ought to live.

week 36

Monday ☐ John 1:1-18
          Luke 1:1-80
Tuesday ☐ Matthew 1:18-25
          Luke 2:1-38
          Matthew 2:1-23
          Luke 2:39-52
Wednesday ☐ Luke 3:1-22
          Matthew 3:1-17
          Mark 1:1-13
          Luke 4:1-13
          Matthew 4:1-11
          John 1:19-34
Thursday ☐ Luke 3:23-38
          Matthew 1:1-17
          John 1:35—3:36
Friday ☐ John 4:1-54
          Luke 4:14-32
          Matthew 4:12-17
          Mark 1:14, 15

Look for:
- Angels, shepherds, kings, and Jesus
- How the Word became flesh
- John, a second Elijah
- Two conversations: Nicodemus and a woman at a well

Jesus' Birth

Almost everything that is known about Jesus' birth is learned from Matthew 1, 2, and Luke 1, 2. Mark says nothing about it, and John explains Jesus' coming philosophically. He calls Him "the Logos," a Greek word that is hard to render adequately. Most versions have it "Word," though "Reason" or "Speech" would also be acceptable. John says this "Logos" (the preexistent Jesus) "became flesh, and lived for awhile among us" (1:14), without telling how this happened.

Matthew's account focuses on Joseph, Jesus' legal father, and Luke's on Mary, His mother. Don't skip over the genealogies (Matthew has Joseph's; Luke has Mary's) just because there are a lot of difficult names in them. Although these lists mean little to us, they were of the utmost importance in establishing that Jesus is who He claimed to be, the Son of David, through both His mother and His earthly father.

Angels

The angel who announced to Mary the coming birth of Jesus, and who probably appeared to Joseph in a dream to ease his mind concerning Mary's condition, was named Gabriel. His name means what he was, "a man of God." He appears four times in the Bible (Daniel 8:16ff; 9:21ff; Luke 1:11ff; 1:26ff). He was probably an archangel, though he is not so called. In addition to Gabriel many other angels are mentioned in this week's readings (see Luke 2:8ff).

People, Places, Circumstances

You'll meet some interesting people this week—Joseph and Mary, Zechariah and Elizabeth, Simeon and Anna, Nicodemus (the scholarly gentleman who had an evening meeting with Jesus) and an unnamed woman from Sychar. And then there is John, who is called the Baptizer. You'll be introduced to him in Luke 1, and see him come to life in Matthew 3 and parallel passages in Mark and Luke. He also plays an important role in John 1, where he testifies to some of his disciples concerning Jesus.

You will get to see Jesus in a lot of different places and circumstances: in Bethlehem, Jerusalem, Cana, and Nazareth; in Judea, Egypt, Galilee, and Samaria; in the wilderness, at the Jordan, by an old well. You will get to see Him in combat with the devil, as a guest at a wedding, as a rejected speaker in a synagogue.

And you'll get to examine the methods Jesus used. He performed miracles, gave intriguing teachings, called disciples, and began to herald abroad the same message John the Baptist was preaching, "The kingdom of God is near" (Mark 1:15).

During the readings for this one week the birth and youth of Jesus are covered. So is the first year of His ministry.

79

week 37

Monday ☐ Luke 5:1-26
Matthew 4:18-25
Mark 1:16—2:12
Luke 4:33-44
Matthew 8:2-17; 9:1-8
Tuesday ☐ Luke 5:27-39
Matthew 9:9-17
Mark 2:13-22
John 5:1-47
Wednesday ☐ Matthew 12:1-21
Mark 2:23—3:19a
Luke 6:1-49
Thursday ☐ Matthew 5:1—8:1
Friday ☐ Luke 7:1-50
Matthew 11:2-30

Look for:
- The Prince of Peace in conflict and controversy
- Fishermen become men-fishers
- Physician, Bridegroom, Teacher
- Happiness expressions for disciples

Ministry in Galilee

About half of Jesus' ministry was in Galilee. He began His work there around January of 28 A.D., and concluded it some 21 months later (October, 29 A.D.) when He attended the Feast of Tabernacles (John 7) in Jerusalem, and remained in Judea for a brief campaign. Not all of that time was spent in Galilee, but much of it was. Both Matthew and Mark devote about half of their books to Jesus' Galilean ministry. Luke, on the other hand, devoted only about one-fourth of his to it, and John, writing much later than the other three, practically ignores it. This week we're going to accompany Jesus as He travels in Galilee and go with Him to Jerusalem to attend a Passover (John 5).

Jesus was a great discipler of men. Notice His method this week as you read about the calling of some fishermen and a publican. Later these same men, plus others, were called into a higher level of discipleship (Mark 3, Luke 6). They became His apostles, those whom He "sent forth" as His representatives.

Capernaum and Nain

Capernaum, on the northwest bank of the Sea of Galilee, was chosen by Jesus as His headquarters city. The name means, "village of Nahum," which may indicate that the prophet Nahum came from there. It appears nowhere in the Bible except in the Gospels. In Jesus' time it must have been a rather important place. As Jesus predicted in Matthew 11:23, 24, the city has vanished; even its site is a matter of dispute.

A village, Nain, fits into this week's material. Beautifully situated on the northwest slope of the Hill of Moreh, it offers a fantastic view. Because of a miracle which Jesus performed there the name of the village will be remembered forever.

Controversies

Sometimes when one reads the Gospels, he feels that Jesus was constantly in a dispute with someone. Notice the times and topics of debate as you read your Scriptures this week. Doesn't it seem strange that people would argue with Him over some of the things they did? "How could they?" we indignantly ask. But then how could we question and doubt as we sometimes do? Surely, if He were here bodily, He would have to contend with us at times!

Miracles

The word "miracle" literally means a marvelous event or an event that causes wonder. Sometimes in the Bible miracles are called wonders, power displays, or signs. Miracles were one of Jesus' specialties; He performed many of them.

When Jesus was in Jerusalem to attend a Passover (John 5), He performed a wonderful miracle at the Pool of Bethesda. The Jews' reaction was that they wanted to kill Him! They didn't; not at this time. What a marvelous message Jesus delivered at this time. What do you think about John 5:28, 29? Doesn't this passage contain a thrilling promise? Check Acts 24:15 and 1 Thessalonians 4:13-18 in connection with it.

The Sermon on the Mount

Is the Sermon on the Plain of Luke 6 the same as the Sermon on the Mount of Matthew 5—7? Not all think so, but there are such striking similarities that most are convinced they are. Couldn't a plain be in a mountain (a plateau)? Actually, it is a great lesson taught by Jesus rather than a sermon preached by Him. It has been called "the Magna Charta of the Kingdom," "the Manifesto of the King," "the Ordination Sermon of the Twelve." What a thrilling and enjoyable passage to read!

week 38

Monday ☐ Matthew 12:22—13:53
Tuesday ☐ Luke 8:1-21
Mark 3:19b—4:34
Wednesday ☐ Matthew 8:18-34; 9:18-34
Mark 4:35—6:6
Matthew 13:54-58
Thursday ☐ Luke 9:57-62
Matthew 9:35—11:1
Mark 6:7-13
Luke 8:22—9:6
Friday ☐ Matthew 14:1-36
Mark 6:14-56
Luke 9:7-17
John 6:1-21

Look for:

- Blasphemy of the Holy Spirit
- Mothers, brothers, and sisters
- Seaside stories
- The Man who talked to storms
    to the insane
    to the dead

The Unforgivable Sin

An awful charge was made against Jesus by the Pharisees. They accused Him of being the devil's partner (Matthew 12, Mark 3). That charge led Jesus to speak about the blasphemy of the Holy Spirit. Students of Scripture are not certain what this is. Many, when they discuss this sin, equate it with the sin mentioned in Hebrews 6:4-8 and 10:26-31. Is John's "sin that leads to death" (1 John 5:16) the same thing?

A "Bad" Day

That day was a "bad" day for Jesus. After the Pharisees saw that He had turned their charge against them, they demanded of Him some sign (Matthew 12:38). Jesus handled that situation with His usual efficiency and dignity. About that time Jesus' mother and brothers showed up and wanted to see Him. From the tone of His words it is obvious their motive was far from pure.

On the other hand note that the "bad" day turned into a good one for Jesus. Matthew 13:1 says: "That same day went Jesus out of the house and sat by the lake." Later He got into a ship, a crowd assembled on the shore and perhaps in other ships, and He taught them what, ever since, have been referred to as the seaside parables. Later that day He gave private instruction to His apostles using this same teaching method.

These events occurred sometime around October or November of 28 A.D. Jesus began His ministry in January of 27, so this means that almost two of the three-and-a-half years of His ministry are behind Him.

A Busy Day

It is not possible to determine which was the busiest day in our Lord's ministry, but the autumn day we are now examining surely deserves consideration. After the above activities Jesus got into a ship and sailed from the northwestern shore of the Sea of Galilee to the eastern shore. On the way He calmed a raging sea, which even the seasoned sailors among His apostles feared. When He and His company arrived on the eastern shore He met, talked with, and freed from Satan's power two men possessed by demons.

Great Events

Later, when Jesus had returned to Capernaum, He was called upon to perform a number of miracles, the most notable of which was the restoration of the life of the daughter of Jairus, a ruler of a local synagogue.

Two other great events happened at this time. About January or February of 29 A.D. Jesus sent out His apostles on a preaching tour of Galilee while He went on His third tour of the area. During this period of intensive evangelism, John the Baptist was put to death. Word of this tragedy was brought to Jesus by John's disciples, who arrived in Capernaum with their sad news about the time the apostles returned from their successful mission. It was therefore a time of mixed emotions for Jesus and His friends.

The other great event, one of the outstanding ones in Jesus' ministry (the first to be recorded by all four Gospels), was the feeding of the 5,000. It took place on the northern shore of the Sea of Galilee in the spring of 29 A.D. John (6:4) says the Passover was near, and in that year the Passover was held on the 17th of April.

week 39

Monday ☐ John 6:22—7:1
Matthew 15:1-28
Mark 7:1-30
Tuesday ☐ Matthew 15:29—18:35
Wednesday ☐ Mark 7:31—9:50
Thursday ☐ Luke 9:18-56
John 7:2-52
Friday ☐ John 7:53—10:21

Look for:
- "You are the Christ"
- Jesus transfigured
- Some of Jesus' "other sheep"
- Money in a fish's mouth
- At the Feast of Tabernacles

Height of Popularity

In April of 29 A.D. Jesus' popularity peaked. Thousands of disciples, both in Judea and especially in Galilee, were solidly behind Him. When He miraculously fed the 5,000 men (besides women and children), His political followers saw great potential in that act. All they had to do was exploit it (share with their fellow Jews that their leader could supply all the food an army needed), and enlarge upon it (imply He could supply anything else that was needed to drive out the Romans and set up the kingdom of David again).

The problem was that Jesus would have no part of such a plan. He never came to establish an earthly kingdom. He had fought with the devil about that in the wilderness temptations, and He wasn't about to alter His plans to suit people who were more interested in the physical than the spiritual. Pay close attention to John 6:66, which portends the collapse of Jesus' campaign.

Confession and Transfiguration

This week you will read about two tremendously important events in Jesus' ministry. The first is Peter's identification of Jesus as "the Christ, the Son of the living God" (Matthew 16:16). That identification by Peter called forth from Jesus His statement that Peter was a rock. What controversy has raged, and continues to do so, over the meaning of Jesus' words in Matthew 16:18!

The second great event is Jesus' transfiguration. It occurred a week after Peter's confession. When it took place, as far as a calendar date is concerned, is unknown. The traditional date is August 6th, 29 A.D. Nor do we know the place, though more than likely it was Mt. Hermon, a mountain a short distance from Caesarea Philippi (where Peter's confession was made). It is indeed a high mountain (Matthew 17:1), rising to 9,400 feet.

Within a period of a few weeks Jesus told His disciples three times of His approaching death. Did the apostles fail to register what He meant because they didn't want to believe such a tragedy was going to befall him? It's amazing how we hear what we want to hear!

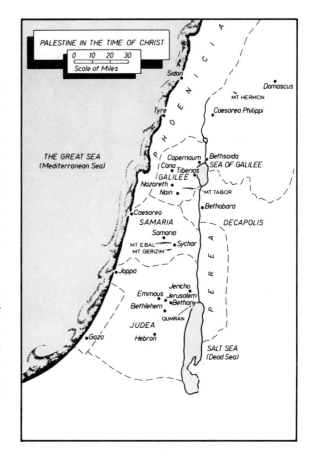

PALESTINE IN THE TIME OF CHRIST

Jesus' Travels

Make a list, a mental one if you can do no better, of the places Jesus visited during this period. Notice that He got into Gentile territory for a while (Phoenicia), where He had an interesting encounter with a woman of faith. If He was on Mt. Hermon, He was in a little country called Abilene. Some time was spent in the Decapolis.

Questions

Many questions will come to mind this week. How did the three apostles recognize Jesus' visitors in the transfiguration scene? How did the money mentioned in Matthew 17:27 get in the fish's mouth? Who was the disciple, unknown to the apostles, who was working miracles? Why didn't Jesus' own brothers believe in Him? Why didn't the "pious" men who brought the adulterous woman also bring the adulterous man?

The Feast of Tabernacles

The Feast of Tabernacles mentioned in John 7 was the one of 29 A.D. This means that Jesus' death was only about six months away! How rapidly His three-and-a-half year ministry flew by. This part of Jesus' ministry, told only by John, provides some thrilling reading.

week 40

Monday ☐ Luke 10, 11
Tuesday ☐ Luke 12, 13
Wednesday ☐ John 10:22-42
Luke 14, 15
Thursday ☐ Luke 16:1—17:10
John 11
Friday ☐ Luke 17:11—19:28

Look for:

- Seventy workers sent out
- A neighborly Samaritan
- The model prayer
- More lessons in parables
- "Lazarus, come out!"
- Ten lepers healed

Jesus in Judea

This week's readings are from Luke and John. Not one of the texts is taken from Matthew or Mark. You will be examining Jesus' later Judean ministry and His Perean ministry (His ministry on the eastern side of the Jordan River). For some reason Matthew and Mark are silent about what Jesus did in and near Jerusalem at the end of 29 and the beginning of 30 A.D., and discuss only a few things about His Perean work. The map (Week 39) will show you where these places are. Don't expect to find the word "Perea" in your Bible; it isn't there. The Jewish historian, Josephus, and others of Jesus' time, used it.

You may recall that Jesus and His disciples came to Jerusalem in October of 29 to attend the Feast of Tabernacles (John 7). He then stayed in the area until the Feast of Dedication (John 10). You can read about the former feast in the Old Testament (Leviticus 23), but not about the latter one. The Feast of Dedication came to be observed by the Jews after the Old Testament writings were completed and before the beginning of Jesus' earthly life. This feast, held in the month Kislev (our December) was instituted by Judas Maccabaeus in 164 B.C. when the temple, which had been defiled, was cleansed and rededicated.

Jesus, the Teacher

Jesus was both preacher and teacher. At times He delivered sermons; at times He taught lessons. Last week's readings included some examples of His sermons (sermon on the Light of the World, John 8:12-59; sermon on the Good Shepherd, John 10:1-21). Now you'll see some more examples of the Master Teacher at work. The parable was His most popular method. Perhaps as many as 40 of them are recorded by Matthew, Mark, and Luke; John records none. This week you are going to read about a dozen of them.

You are going to be exposed to some very practical and important teaching this week. You will learn about prayer, repentance, the cost of discipleship, little children, the problems of having riches, and the rewards God intends for His followers.

Jesus' Friends

Some of Jesus' closest friends were the folks from Bethany—Lazarus and his sisters Mary and Martha. Lazarus means "God has helped," a fitting name for this man whom Jesus restored to life. This lovely family comes into the readings a couple of times this week. Also, a new acquaintance is made by Jesus—a man named Zaccheus.

Jesus surely had His friends, devoted ones. He also had His enemies, and He didn't hesitate to denounce them. Have you ever wondered who He would denounce if He walked our streets today?

Thoughtlessness

Jesus was often hurting. That was because He cared so much and because some seemed not to care at all! It must have been a bitter pill when, after healing ten lepers, only one of them returned and said thanks. Think as you read this week of other deeds and words that must have caused Him pain. Some thought should also be given as to how our actions and expressions harm Him.

week 41

Monday ☐ Matthew 19:1—20:34
Tuesday ☐ Mark 10:1-52
Wednesday ☐ John 12:1-19
Luke 19:29—20:44
Thursday ☐ Matthew 26:6-13
Matthew 21:1—22:46
Friday ☐ Mark 14:3-9
Mark 11:1—12:37

Look for:

- Words about divorce
- A young rich man
- Two of the "inner circle" rebuked
- Triumphal ride into Jerusalem
- The day the questions were asked

Marriage and Divorce

Marriage is from God, is not to be entered lightly, and is to be dissolved only as a last resort and under specific conditions. Jesus spoke of marriage in Matthew 19 (Mark 10) and also in Matthew 5. Paul also spoke of it. In Ephesians 5 he presented the relationship that Christ bears to the church as a model for the relationship that husbands should bear to their wives.

Jesus in Jericho

Jesus' teaching in Matthew 19 was given while Jesus was in Perea. He left there, crossed the Jordan, entered Jericho, and there had an encounter with two blind men and another with Zaccheus. In March of 30 A.D. Jesus left Perea with His face steadfastly set toward Jerusalem, where He was prepared to offer himself as the perfect Lamb of God.

In Bethany

John says that Jesus arrived in Bethany six days before the Passover (12:1). That would make it the Friday before His crucifixion. Accepting April 7th as the day of Jesus' death, then His arrival at Bethany would have been on March 31st.

At a supper held on Saturday evening, Mary of Bethany aroused the indignation of Judas and others by anointing Jesus' body with costly ointment. The spikenard she used is a rose-red fragrant ointment made from the dried roots and woolly stems of a plant by the same name. It was imported into Palestine from northern India, and hence was very expensive. It was in an alabaster container, a jar made out of a special kind of stone.

In Jerusalem

The triumphal entry is recorded by all four Gospel writers, only the second event in Jesus' life, up until this time, to have this distinction. It occurred on Sunday, April 2nd.

Jesus made Bethany (sometimes called His Judean home) His headquarters for the last week of His life. From there a footpath led to Jerusalem, and apparently Jesus took this route on His triumphant ride.

It was also along this path that He saw and cursed a fig tree because it bore no figs. This event must have taken place on Monday of "Passion Week," and was followed by the second cleansing of the temple.

The Great Day of Questions

Tuesday was one of the tremendous days in Jesus' life. Viewed as to the number of known events in which He became engaged, it qualifies as His busiest day, surpassing even the one on which He taught the seaside parables. In Matthew's Gospel four entire chapters and portions of two others are devoted to it.

Activity followed activity on this hectic day, as Jesus taught and preached under the pressure of realizing that the time of His death was fast approaching.

This day, called by some, "The Great Day of Questions," well deserves the name. There was a question about tribute to Caesar, one

about the resurrection, another about the greatest commandment, and yet another about the Son of David. The first three were asked of Jesus by His enemies who hoped to ensnare Him in His speech. To each question Jesus gave a correct and adequate answer. But to *His* question, concerning the Son of David, no answer was given. Matthew observes: "From that day on no one dared to ask him any more questions" (22:46).

week

42

Monday ☐ Matthew 23:1-39
         Mark 12:38-44
         Luke 20:45—21:4
         John 12:20-50
Tuesday ☐ Matthew 24
         Mark 13
         Luke 21:5-38
Wednesday ☐ Matthew 25:1—26:5;
         26:14-35
         Mark 14:1, 2, 10-31
Thursday ☐ Luke 22:1-38
         John 13
Friday ☐ John 14—17

Look for:
- The destruction of Jerusalem and the end of the world
- Sheep and goats
- The last supper
- Jesus' high priestly prayer

Jesus' Speech

At times Jesus said some harsh things. He called the Pharisees, religious leaders of His time, children of Hell, blind guides, fools, whitewashed tombs, serpents, and vipers. He accused them of being hypocrites, play actors, people who faked their religion. At other times He said very kind, gracious things. As an example, He commended a widow who gave two small copper coins, worth only a fraction of a penny, to God. Always what He said was true, and always it was intriguing. This week's reading includes several selections of the latter variety.

Eschatology

Most students of the Bible are fascinated by what it says about the last days and final things. The formal word for such a study is *eschatology*. Such a study includes the topics of death, resurrection, the return of Christ, the end of the world, divine judgment, and the future life.

Students of eschatology are in for a real treat this week. You will read Jesus' sermon on the significance of life and death (John 12:20-50), the parable of the ten virgins and the parable of the talents (Matthew 25:1-30—both dealing with Christ's return), His discussion concerning judgment (Matthew 25:31-46), plus (and this is really an enticing one)

His words in Matthew 24, Mark 13, and Luke 21 about the fall of Jerusalem, His second coming, and the end of the world!

All of these events happened on the Tuesday of Jesus' last week. Wednesday Jesus apparently rested.

The Betrayal and the Last Supper

Why did Judas betray His Lord? It's a hard question to answer. (Don't answer that he had to do so in order to fulfill prophecy. If you do, you are taking Judas' responsibility from him.) Jesus knew it was going to happen and warned Judas about it.

Because He did not want the last supper interrupted, Jesus was cautious and secretive about where it would be eaten. A lot of things happened at that meal, but nothing more important than the instituting of the Lord's Supper. Whether or not Judas was still present to eat that special meal is difficult to determine from the texts.

John, who alone tells about the washing of the disciples' feet, is also the only Gospel writer to record Jesus' wonderful farewell address when He spoke of His Father's house and of His return for His own (John 14), the parable of the vine (John 15), His grave instructions (John 16), and His great priestly prayer (John 17).

The prayer in John 17 should be read often. Through it can be gained an insight into the heart of Jesus such as no other text affords. Notice His grave concern for the unity of His followers. "My prayer is not for them alone. I pray also for those who will believe in me through their message, that all of them may be one, Father, just as you are in me and I am in you. May they also be in us so that the world may believe that you have sent me" (17:20, 21).

week 43

Monday ☐ John 18:1—19:42
Tuesday ☐ Matthew 26:36—27:66
Wednesday ☐ Luke 22:39—23:56
　　　　　Matthew 28:1-20
Thursday ☐ Mark 14:32—16:20
Friday ☐ Luke 24
　　　　　John 20, 21

Look for:
- "Not as I will, but as you will"
- The six trials of Jesus
- Denied by Peter
- Seven words from the cross
- Buried in another's tomb
- Jesus—alive and well

The Garden of Gethsemane

Sometime on Thursday evening, perhaps as early as 8:00 P.M., but possibly as late as midnight, Jesus and His apostles entered the Garden of Gethsemane. There Jesus poured out His heart to the Heavenly Father, and through prayer, steeled himself for the activities of "Good Friday." Perhaps about 1:00 A.M. He was arrested and taken off to be tried.

Six Trials

Jesus appeared before four men in His six trials: Annas, Caiaphas, Pilate, and Herod. Annas served as high priest from A.D. 7 to 15. After his removal from office he succeeded in getting the office for five of his sons as well as Caiaphas, his son-in-law. Caiaphas, also called Joseph, served from 18-36. He was the reigning high priest during the trials of Jesus.

Little is known about Pilate. His procuratorship lasted for ten years (27-37). In addition to the references to him in the Gospels, he is mentioned three times in Acts (3:13; 4:27; 13:28).

Herod Antipas was the son of Herod the Great and Malthace, a Samaritan woman. He ruled over Galilee and Perea as tetrarch from his father's death until 39 A.D.

These men, whose names are household words among Christians, became infamous because of their part in the crucifixion of God's Son.

Some Roman soldiers used Jesus'

claim to be the King of the Jews as the basis of fun-making at His expense. They put on Him a scarlet robe and a crown of thorns, and placed a reed in His right hand to be His scepter. They also smote Him with a reed and spat on Him.

The Crucifixion

After that He was led out to Golgotha (Hebrew) or Calvary (Latin), words that mean, "the skull," and crucified.

On the cross He spoke seven times. The order of His utterances is a topic for debate. Many hold the order to be: "Father, forgive them, for they do not know what they are doing" (Luke 23:34); "I tell you the truth, today you will be with me in paradise" (Luke 23:43); "Dear woman, here is your son. . . . Here is your mother" (John 19:26, 27); "My God, my God, why have you forsaken me?" (Matthew 27:46; Mark 15:34); "I am thirsty" (John 19:28): "It is finished" (John 19:30); "Father, into your hands I commit my spirit" (Luke 23:46).

The Burial

Who was Joseph of Arimathea, in whose tomb Jesus was buried? John says he was a secret disciple (19:38), and Luke tells us he was a counsellor (member of the Sanhedrin), a good and just man (23:50). Arimathea is usually equated with a place called Rama, in the territory of Benjamin, near Jerusalem.

The Resurrection

Christ's resurrection occurred on April 9th. No one witnessed it, so the exact procedure is unknown. Sometime after the resurrection Jesus appeared to Mary Magdalene, then to some other women. Later that same day He appeared to two disciples as they traveled to a place called Emmaus, to Simon Peter, and to ten of the apostles in an upper room in Jerusalem.

During the next forty days Jesus made several other appearances: to the eleven, to seven by the Sea of Galilee, to 500 in Galilee, to other disciples in Jerusalem, to James the Lord's brother, and to the disciples once again. His ascension took place at Bethany. Luke says He was carried up into Heaven (24:51); Mark, that He was received up (16:19); and the Acts passage that He was taken up (KJV). The Acts passage is the most complete of the three. Note what the angels said in Acts: Jesus is coming "in the same way" as He went into Heaven (1:11). And someday He will, praise God!

week 44

Monday ☐ Acts 1—3
Tuesday ☐ Acts 4, 5
Wednesday ☐ Acts 6:1—8:1
Thursday ☐ Acts 8:2—9:31
Galatians 1:17-24
Friday ☐ Acts 9:32—11:18
Acts 12:1-24
Acts 11:19-30; 12:25

Look for:
- The birthday of the church
- Peter and John arrested
- Death of two deceivers
- Work of Stephen and Philip
- Conversions of Saul
  and Cornelius

The Author of Acts

Luke, the author of Acts, has been called a "historian par excellence." He was a meticulous researcher (see Luke 1:1-4) and a careful user of words (this can be seen especially when he describes Roman officials), who enriched his writing with terminology from his medical profession, and whose use of nautical terms has endeared him to sailors of all times.

Luke, Paul's companion at times (see Acts 16:10-17; 20:5—21:18; 27:1—28:16) was a Gentile. Either he was from Antioch of Syria (an old tradition) or from Philippi. He was with Paul during his Roman imprisonment, and completed his history after Paul had "dwelt two whole years in his own hired house" (28:30). This would place the writing of Acts in 63 A.D.

Jesus' Work Continues

The Gospels inform us of the things "Jesus began to do and to teach until the day he was taken up to heaven" (Acts 1:1, 2). Acts relates the continuing work of Jesus both directly and through the Holy Spirit and His apostles. In fact, the Holy Spirit plays such a dominant role in this 28-chapter book that it would be fitting to call it, "The Acts of the

Holy Spirit," rather than "The Acts of the Apostles," its more popular name. The original manuscript carried no title.

Some believe that Acts 1:8 contains a general outline of the book: "Ye shall be witnesses unto me both in Jerusalem, and in all Judea, and in Samaria and unto the uttermost part of the earth." Not a lot is said about the expansion of the work in Judea (although it is indicated in 8:1), but the other three areas are well represented. Chapters 1—7 center around Jerusalem, 8—12 deal with the work in Judea and Samaria, and 13—28 present the church's expansion unto "the ends of the earth."

The Book's Main Characters

Although long called, "The Acts of the Apostles," it would be more appropriate to refer to it as "Some of the Acts of the Some of the Apostles." Specifically, it is a book dealing with some of the works of Peter and Paul. The former is the "star" in the first 12 chapters, the latter in the last 16. Those with supporting roles are John, two Jameses, Stephen, Philip, Barnabas, Apollos, Timothy, Aquila and Priscilla, and others. The political figures in the book are Sergius Paulus, Gallio, Claudius Lysias, Felix, Festus, Herod Agrippa I and II, and Julius.

Another thing to note about the book is the number of speeches it contains. There are 24 of them—nine by Peter, nine by Paul, plus one by each of the following: Gamaliel, Stephen, James, Demetrius, a town clerk, and Festus, the Roman governor.

Galatians

This week you will be briefly introduced to the book of Galatians. The reason is apparent—the passage to be read (1:17-24) provides further insight into Paul's activities. The rest of the book will be read later.

week 45

Monday ☐ Acts 13:1—14:28
Tuesday ☐ Acts 15:1-35
Galatians 2
Acts 15:36—16:10
Wednesday ☐ Acts 16:11—18:18a
1 Thessalonians 1
Thursday ☐ 1 Thessalonians 2—5
2 Thessalonians 1—3
Friday ☐ Acts 18:18b—19:22
1 Corinthians 1—3

Look for:
- Paul sent as a missionary
- Jerusalem Conference
- An earthquake in prison
- Words about the Lord's return
- Wood, hay, and straw

Paul, Traveler and Writer

Understanding Acts will provide one with a background for Paul's epistles. In this book of history Paul, the dominant character of chapters 13—28, is seen moving about the Roman world preaching and teaching and establishing churches wherever possible. He addressed his epistles to congregations he established, individuals he converted, and people with whom he labored. In fact, the writing of his letters occurred while he was on his journeys. Determining where Paul was when he wrote specific letters makes for an interesting study. In your readings for the next few weeks you will be alternating between the epistles and Acts, hopefully seeing the rationale for the particular arrangement.

The First Missionary Journey

Acts covers three of Paul's missionary journeys plus his trip to Rome as a prisoner. The first trip is covered in Acts 13:1—14:28. It lasted about four years (45-49) and involved Barnabas and John Mark. It began at Antioch of Syria, and included stops on the island of Cyprus, in the province of Pamphylia, in Pisidia (in the region of southern Galatia), and in Lycaonia. It ended with Paul's and Barnabas's return to Antioch.

The Second Journey

After sharing in a conference held in Jerusalem regarding circumcision (Acts 15), Paul left on his second tour (Acts 15:36—18:22). With Silas as his assistant, Paul moved northward

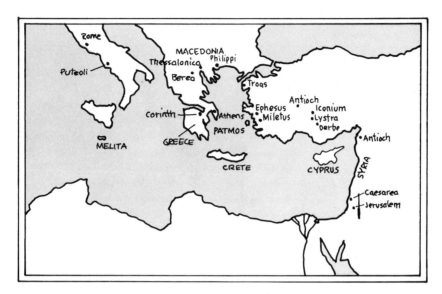

from Antioch of Syria through Cilicia into southern Galatia, and revisited the churches that he had established in Lycaonia and Pisidia. Acquiring a new helper, Timothy, in Lystra, Paul and his party moved westward to the coast of Asia Minor. There, at Troas, Paul was joined by Luke (16:11), and in obedience to a vision from God they sailed across the Aegean Sea and began evangelizing the European continent. They worked first in Macedonia, and then in Achaia.

Recrossing the Aegean Sea, Paul stopped briefly in Ephesus before going on to Caesarea and then to Antioch to report to the church that had commissioned him. The years 50-53 were spent on this journey.

The Third Journey

Paul's third journey began from Antioch in 54 A.D. (Acts 18:23), and ended with his arrest in Jerusalem in 58 (Acts 21). Leaving Antioch Paul traveled westward again and came to Ephesus. After a stay of some three years, Paul revisited Europe and then went to Caesarea in Palestine. From there he went to Jerusalem, where he was arrested. Thus began a period of some five years in which Paul was kept in confinement. Acts ends with Paul still a prisoner.

The Thessalonian Letters

Paul's work in Thessalonica is described in Acts 17. As was his custom, he began his labors there with fellow Jews in a local synagogue (17:2), but reached out to others as well (v. 3).

After leaving Thessalonica Paul went to Berea, and then to Greece to work in both Athens and Corinth. It is generally agreed that Paul, while at Corinth, wrote both of the Thessalonian letters. This was about 53 A.D., which means these are Paul's earliest letters. They are called his "eschatological epistles" because they have so much to say about Christ's return.

week

46

Monday ☐ 1 Corinthians 4—8
Tuesday ☐ 1 Corinthians 9—11
Wednesday ☐ 1 Corinthians 12—14
Thursday ☐ 1 Corinthians 15, 16
Friday ☐ Acts 19:23—20:1
2 Corinthians 1:1—4:6

Look for:
- The temple of the Holy Spirit
- How to observe the Lord's Supper
- Love
- Resurrection

Paul in Corinth

On his second missionary journey Paul began the church in Corinth. Luke's account of this phase of Paul's endeavors is found in Acts 18, which you read last week. Paul spent a year and half (52, 53 A.D.) in Corinth before he ended his second journey by returning to Antioch (18:22).

Two-sea'd Corinth, as it was called, was located on an isthmus between the Peloponnesus and the mainland. Because of its excellent geographical location it was a ctiy of great commercial importance. A city was founded there before 1000 B.C., but because of rebellion by its citizens it was destroyed by the Romans in 146 B.C. The new city, the one visited by Paul, was rebuilt as a Roman colony by Julius Caesar in 46 B.C. It was a city of wealth and luxury, but also of great immorality. One writer says it had no rival as a city of vice. The citizens worshiped Aphrodite, goddess of love, and a thousand priestesses who were devoted to her functioned as religious prostitutes.

The Letters

Paul had a lengthy ministry in Ephesus on his third journey. There he wrote 1 Corinthians, in response to a letter he had received (1 Corinthians 7:1). Soon afterward he left Ephesus, sailed into Macedonia.

Second Corinthians was written by Paul from somewhere in Macedonia, in about 57 A.D. Some early manuscript subscriptions indicate Philippi was the place of writing, and that may be true. It was written some seven or eight months after 1 Corinthians, and follows up on some things introduced in the earlier letter. Compare 1 Corinthians 16:1, 2 with 2 Corinthians 8 and 9, and 1 Corinthians 5 with 2 Corinthians 2.

The Problem Church

The Corinthian church is often spoken of as "the problem church." Indeed it deserved that title. There was a problem of division (chapters 1—3), of fornication (5), of lawsuits pitting brother against brother (6), an indifference to the conscience of the weak (8—10), disorder at the Lord's Table (11), and confusion regarding the use of spiritual gifts (12—14).

But it was also a church that possessed certain virtues. One of these was its willingness to comply with the counsel offered by the inspired Paul (see 2 Corinthians 7:6-11). There was also a loyalty to the truth of the gospel. Paul speaks of the members "standing in the truth" (1 Corinthians 15:1).

First Corinthians provides an insight into early church life and worship, contains the famous "love chapter" (13), and has the most complete discussion of the resurrected state to be found in the Bible (15). It also provides us a precedent for the paid ministry (9) and the weekly offering (16). Marriage is also discussed.

week 47

Monday ☐ 2 Corinthians 4:7—9:15
Tuesday ☐ 2 Corinthians 10—13
Wednesday ☐ James 1—5
Thursday ☐ Acts 20:1-3a
Romans 1—4
Friday ☐ Romans 5—8

Look for:
- A glimpse into Paul's life
- Christian stewardship
- Advice on prejudice, speech, and the world
- Faith and actions
- Dead to sin

A Personal Book

Second Corinthians is recognized as an intensely personal book, "Paul's apology for his life," as one has called it. It will give you some good insights into the character of the great apostle. It also contains material that is doctrinal and practical (see 2:5-11; 3; 6:11—7:10; 8; 9; 13).

Paul, after sending 1 Corinthians by Titus, suffered a great deal of concern as to whether the church would accept his words of correction. It must have been a joyful time for Paul when, somewhere in Macedonia, he met Titus and received an encouraging report of how the Corinthian church had responded. Out of this background he wrote 2 Corinthians.

The General Epistles

James (and also the epistles of Peter, John, and Jude) are classed as general epistles. This means they were not addressed to individual churches or persons, but to the church in general. (Actually, this doesn't hold true for 2 and 3 John, but still the term is applied to them.)

James

This wonderful five-chapter book, written by the half-brother of Jesus (Matthew 13:55), is the most Jewish sounding book in the New Testament. Still, the spirit of the letter, as well as two references to Christ, makes it clear that this book is truly a Christian epistle. It is addressed to "the twelve tribes scattered among the nations," which may refer to Jewish Christians living outside the

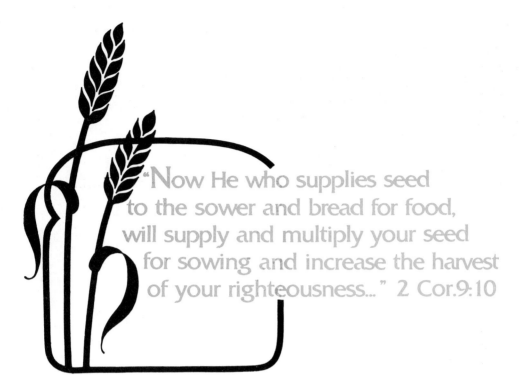

"Now He who supplies seed to the sower and bread for food, will supply and multiply your seed for sowing and increase the harvest of your righteousness..." 2 Cor. 9:10

homeland, though other interpretations of the phrase are possible.

Just when James wrote his little jewel is impossible to say. There are advocates for a very early date (in the latter half of the forties), and some advocates for a date in the sixties, just before James' death.

A Perfect Man

As can be detected from a mere reading of James, this epistle is informal in its structure, making an outlining of it difficult. What we have is a series of warnings, instructions, and exhortations about living the moral and religious life. James wants his readers to do what the Word says, and not merely listen (1:22).

In 3:2 James speaks about "a perfect man." That is really what the book is all about—how to be a per-

fect man. As you read the book this week search out the various areas in which this perfection is to be seen. For instance, in chapter one James indicates a man should be perfect (complete, mature) in the way he handles trials and temptations. Discover the other ways he says the Christian should have this maturity.

James and Paul

Although James and Paul are sometimes set in conflict by some writers, there is no difference between the doctrine of these two men. Paul speaks *for* faith as the principle of salvation, and against works as the basis of a person's redemption. James, on the other hand, insists upon works as the proof that he has the faith which he professes. Paul, in urging Christian conduct in his epistles, says the same thing James does.

week 48

Monday ☐ Romans 9—11
Tuesday ☐ Romans 12—16
Wednesday ☐ Galatians 1:1-17; 3—6
Thursday ☐ Acts 20:3b—22:29
Friday ☐ Acts 22:30—25:27

Look for:
- Practical advice about Christian living
- Only one gospel
- Arrest in Jerusalem
- Paul testifies before priest, governor, and king

Paul's Third Journey

Acts 20:2, 3 tell how Paul, on his third missionary journey, spent three months in Greece before traveling through Macedonia on his way to Jerusalem. It is generally accepted that both Galatians and Romans were written during this three-month period. The year was 58 A.D. These books have a number of similarities, perhaps the greatest being their strong emphasis upon justification by faith instead of works.

The "Fighting Epistle"

Galatians has been called Paul's fighting epistle. He wrote the book to preserve the purity of the gospel and hence warned against those who would preach "another gospel." This book became the battle cry of the reformation; it is frequently cited as Martin Luther's favorite epistle. There is a sternness about the letter; Paul neither expresses thankfulness nor requests prayers. Neither does he offer any words of praise.

The "Greatest Epistle"

Many refer to Romans as the greatest of Paul's epistles. Some call it the greatest book in the New Testament, which would make it the greatest book in the Bible! Why is it so lauded? What makes it so great? It is great in both its subject matter and style of writing. Be on the lookout for these qualities as this week you read chapters 9—16. As you read, remember you are reading a *letter* from Paul to a church he had never visited, but was looking forward to visiting.

The following is a good, simple outline of the book:

1. The gospel and salvation (chapters 1—8)
2. The gospel and Israel (chapters 9—11)
3. The gospel and Christian living (chapters 12—16)

Paul's Arrest

After the three-month stay in Greece, during which time Paul wrote Galatians and Romans, he made a rather hurried trip northward through Macedonia and then southward along the Asian coast of the Aegean Sea on his way to Caesarea and Jerusalem. He wanted to arrive in Jerusalem by the day of Pentecost (Acts 20:16). Along the way "in every city" Paul was warned by the Holy Spirit that "prison and hardships" awaited him.

After his arrival in Jerusalem and a brief time there, he was arrested as predicted. For the next five years he was kept a prisoner first in one place and then another. About two years of this time was spent in Caesarea, where Paul appeared before Ananias, the high priest, Tertullus, an orator, Felix, the Roman governor (and his wife, Drusilla), Festus, who was Felix's replacement, and Herod Agrippa II (and his wife/consort, Bernice). As you read about these people be certain to notice how Paul, the prisoner, supposedly defending his own life, regularly took advantage of the opportunities given him to preach about Jesus. With great skill he turned the tables and placed his audiences on trial before the highest of all tribunals, the judgment seat of God.

week 49

Monday ☐ Acts 26—28
Tuesday ☐ Philemon
          Ephesians 1—3
Wednesday ☐ Ephesians 4—6
Thursday ☐ Philippians 1—4
Friday ☐ Colossians 1—4

Look for:
- Paul, prisoner in Rome
- Unity of the church
- "Rejoice in the Lord"
- "Seek those things which are above"

Paul in Rome

Paul had an intense desire to visit Rome. He made that clear in the first chapter of the Roman letter (1:11-15). It was apparently his intention to get there as he had gotten to other places, through gifts of God's people and his own labor. However, through God's providence and the courts of Rome he was given a free trip, as a prisoner!

He arrived in 61 A.D. and was in Rome for at least two years (Acts 28:30). This period of confinement was not a time of idleness for Paul. He used the time to write four of the epistles in our New Testament—Colossians, Philemon, Ephesians, and Philippians (though not necessarily in that order).

Ephesians

Ephesians was written to a church where Paul had had, for him, a lengthy ministry, one of about three years. This was while he was on his third journey.

Paul's purpose in writing this letter seems to have been to set forth God's eternal plan of redemption in Christ Jesus. Notice verses 1:9, 10, which speak of the summing up of all things, things in Heaven and things upon earth, in Christ. Chapters 1—3 are doctrinal (the church and God's plan of redemption), while 4—6 are practical (what God's plan calls the church to do).

Colossians

As far as is known, Paul was never in Colosse. He journeyed near it more than once (Acts 16:6; 19:1), and

lived within 100 miles of it, at Ephesus, for three years, but never seems to have gone there. Instead, people from there went to Ephesus, heard Paul, and were converted and trained by him. Notice Acts 19:10.

The book has a doctrinal section (1:1—2:3), which sets forth the nature and person of Christ; an apologetic section, in which Paul argues against certain heretical ideas which had crept into the church (2:4—3:4), a practical section (3:5—4:6), and the usual personal section, in which Paul greeted and sent greetings (4:7-18).

Philippians

Philippians is often called Paul's epistle of joy, joy in Christ being mentioned in each of its four chapters. It was written by Paul to his first European church, a congregation that included a businesswoman, Lydia, an unnamed jailer, and perhaps a maiden whom Paul released from the devil's power.

When Paul was in Rome, Epaphroditus was sent with a gift for him from the Philippian Christians. When he made ready to return, Paul sent this letter with him. This was about 63 A.D.

Some of the key verses of Philippians are 1:21, 2:5, 3:10, and 4:13. This last verse, which says, "I can do everything through him who gives me strength," could well be the motto of every Christian.

Philemon

Philemon, a wealthy man of Colosse, was a convert of Paul. Like many wealthy men in the Roman Empire, he was a slaveowner, one who did not feel that it was inconsistent for him, as a Christian, to have slaves. Onesimus, one of his slaves, stole from him, and then ran away to Rome where he met and was converted by Paul. This letter was sent with Onesimus as he returned to his owner. It is Paul's attempt to reconcile master and slave. Although we do not know the results of the letter, it is assumed that Philemon accepted Onesimus as a brother, in answer to Paul's appeal.

week 50

Monday ☐ Hebrews 1—6
Tuesday ☐ Hebrews 7—10
Wednesday ☐ Hebrews 11—13
Thursday ☐ 1 Peter 1—5
Friday ☐ 2 Peter 1—3

Look for:
- Christianity, better in every way
- Earthly pictures of heavenly realities
- Examples of faith
- An incorruptible inheritance

Hebrews

"Who wrote the epistle (to the Hebrews) in truth God alone knows." Such were the sentiments of Origen, the early church father, and such have been the convictions of most other students of this intriguing book. Several indications in the book point to Paul (be on the lookout for these hints as you read), but there is far from unanimity in attributing the book to him. Others frequently suggested include Barnabas, Luke, and especially, Apollos. Who did the writing is not as important as who directed the writing, the Holy Spirit. His mark can be seen throughout.

The heading, "To the Hebrews," was not a part of the original manuscript, yet it is generally accepted that the book was intended for Jewish Christians, probably those living in Palestine. It is clear that it is not one of the earlier epistles because the recipients were second-generation Christians. The suggested date of the book is 63, and the place of writing, Italy (see 13:24).

Purpose of Hebrews

Two purposes can be seen in the book: (1) to show the superiority of Christianity over Judaism; and (2) to keep the Jewish Christians from giving up their faith and returning to the law of Moses.

"Better" is a key word throughout the book's 13 chapters. We Christians have a better revelation, hope, priesthood, covenant, promises, sacrifices, country, and revelation than Jews under the Mosaic dispensation had. "Let us" is another key phrase.

It is used eleven times in the book. Be on the lookout for this expression.

The book can be outlined in the following way:

1. Christ is superior to angels, Moses and Joshua, and Aaron (1:1—5:10)
2. Christianity is superior because it has a superior priesthood, covenant, and sacrifice/ministry (7:1—10:18)
3. Christians are superior because they have received the promise, been disciplined as sons, and come to Mt. Zion (11:1—12:29)

Following each of these sections is a passage exhorting the recipients to remain faithful to their profession of faith.

One of the most popular chapters in the book is the eleventh, the faith chapter of the Bible. It defines and illustrates faith.

Peter's Epistles

Peter wrote his two epistles sometime during the 60's. First Peter is usually assigned to 64, and 2 Peter to 67. The first is addressed to "strangers" scattered throughout Asia Minor (which probably means Christians in general, for whom this world is not home), and the second to Christians possessing the same precious faith Peter had. Suffering is stressed in the first letter (1:6, 7, 11; 2:19-21; 3:9, 14; 4:12, 14, 15, 19; 5:1), and false teachers and teaching in the second (1:16; chapter 2; 3:3, 4, 17). Both end with an emphasis upon the return of Christ (1 Peter 3:13ff; 2 Peter 3). From both books shines a ray of hope.

Here is a suggested outline:

1 Peter
  The Christian's hope (1:1—2:10)
  The Christian's life (2:11—4:11)
  The return of the Christian's Shepherd (4:12—5:14)
2 Peter
  Christian virtues (1:1-14)
  The holy Scriptures (1:15-21)
  False teachers and teaching (2)
  The return of Christ (3)

week 51

Monday ☐ 1 Timothy 1—6
Tuesday ☐ Titus 1—3
Wednesday ☐ 2 Timothy 1—4
Thursday ☐ 1 John 1—5
Friday ☐ 2 John
3 John
Jude

Look for:

- Warning from the Holy Spirit
- Advice about Christian conduct
- Walking in the light
- Walking in love

Seven Letters

Three of this week's books were written by Paul (1 and 2 Timothy, Titus), three by John (1, 2, 3 John), and one by Jude, half-brother of Jesus and full-brother of the James who wrote the epistle by that name. All are brief; three of them have only one chapter, and the longest only six. From the end of the 18th century Paul's three have been called "the pastoral epistles," an incorrect title, since the letters are addressed to men who were evangelists, not pastors. Still, they do deal with the oversight of the church, and to that extent are correctly named.

1 and 2 Timothy

It seems that 1 Timothy was written after Paul's release from his first Roman imprisonment, probably in 64 A.D., and 2 Timothy a couple of years later, during Paul's second confinement in Rome, the one that led to his martyrdom.

Timothy, the recipient, was one of Paul's closest friends. He is first mentioned in Acts 16 and regularly thereafter throughout Paul's travels and in his letters. According to one writer, his name appears 24 times in the Bible—in Acts, Romans, 1 and 2 Corinthians, Philippians, 1 Thessalonians, and Hebrews, as well as in both the letters that bear his name. We know his mother's and grandmother's names, but not his Gentile father's (1 Timothy 1:5).

Titus

Paul's letter to Titus, his "partner and fellow worker" (2 Corinthians

8:23), was probably written soon after 1 Timothy, perhaps in 65 A.D. In its three chapters Titus, who had been left on the island of Crete, was instructed by Paul concerning church life (chapter 1), family and personal life (chapter 2), and public life (chapter 3). Among other attractions in the book are the qualifications for the office of bishop or elder (Titus 1; see also 1 Timothy 3).

John's Epistles

Sometimes between 85-90 A.D. John wrote his three little epistles. The first one bears the name of no specific recipent(s), but like the Gospel of John, it has a philosophical introduction. In fact there are no proper names (except the Lord's), in the book, nor are there any references to history or geography. It is a book of warnings against false teachers and of exhortations to be true to the Christian faith. "We know" is one of its key expressions, appearing more than 30 times.

By way of contrast, both 2 and 3 John, like the usual Greek letter, have salutations. Second John is addressed to "the chosen lady and her children" (a phrase that is subject to several interpretations), and 3 John to a "dear friend" named Gaius. Each of these letters evidently was written to fit on a single sheet of papyrus, hence the similar size. Second John speaks of walking in truth and love, a worthy goal for all Christians. Third John is like a drama (and indeed it describes a real-life one) with three characters: Gaius, the star, who walked in the truth, Diotrephes, the villain, who loved to have preeminence, and Demetrius, a supporting actor, who had a good report of all men.

Jude

Jude, a book of 25 verses, probably was written sometime after 2 Peter, to which it is similar, perhaps in 68 or 69 A.D. It harshly denounces false teachers (5-16), reminds Christians of their responsibilities (17-23), and concludes with a beautiful doxology.

week 52

Monday ☐ Revelation 1—3
Tuesday ☐ Revelation 4—9
Wednesday ☐ Revelation 10—14
Thursday ☐ Revelation 15—18
Friday ☐ Revelation 19—22

Look for:
- A vision of Jesus
- Letters to churches
- Sevens
- The marriage of the Lamb
- A new Heaven and earth

John's Fifth Book

Revelation is the fifth book from the pen of John, the beloved apostle. The title means an unveiling, a revealing of things that are covered. The first three verses of the book help explain its purpose. So does verse 1:19. The setting for the writing of the book is given in 1:9; John is "on the island of Patmos because of the word of God and the testimony of Jesus." John's exile was probably during the reign of Domitian (81-96), and therefore an accepted date for this book is 95 or 96 A.D.

Revelation is an apocalyptical book, and is similar to Ezekiel, Daniel, and Zechariah. Because of its nature it is not easy to understand. Yet, since the book was designed as an "uncovering" there are surely many truths that can and should be gleaned from it. Some find it the most difficult book of the Bible to understand; it is surely one of the most controversial.

There are four general schools of thought about the book, each advocating a different approach. Preterists (from Latin, for past), hold that most of the prophecies of the book have already been fulfilled. Futurists hold just the opposite view, believing that the book deals principally with the end time, the consummation of the age. Those who advocate the continuous-historical position believe that the book offers an unfolding of the entire history of the church from John's time until the end times. The fourth, the spiritual view, is that the book is figurative, that it employs symbols to show the triumph of good over evil, and that the principles revealed in the book continue to work in all of history. The position one holds greatly influences how he interprets the book.

Main Topics

Following an eight-verse introduction, chapter 1 contains Jesus' self-revelation to John on Patmos. Chapters 2 and 3 present the seven letters to the churches in Asia Minor. Seven seals are mentioned in 4:1 to 8:1, and seven trumpets in 8:2 to 11:18. There are seven persons in 11:19—14:20, and chapters 15 and 16 describe seven bowls of wrath. In chapters 17 and 18 the fall of Babylon is pictured. Chapter 19 deals with the marriage supper of the Lamb, and in chapter 20 a millennium (a thousand-year period) is described (this is a highly controversial chapter). Eternity, with its Heaven and Hell, is portrayed in the last two chapters (21:1—22:5), followed by the book's conclusion.

End of the Bible

This book, and hence the Bible as we have it arranged, ends with an invitation from the Spirit and the bride (v. 17), a fearful warning to those who would tamper with its contents (vv. 18, 19), with the appeal of John, "Amen. Come, Lord Jesus," and with the blessed words, "The grace of the Lord Jesus be with God's people. Amen."

RESOURCES
for Bible Reading and Study

Selecting a Translation of the Bible by Dr. Lewis Foster
   Why so many translations of the Bible? How do you tell which translation works best for which purpose? The author reviews ten of the most popular Bible translations available today.
   This book will help you in selecting a translation of the Bible, whether for study, for devotional reading, or for pulpit or pew **(39975).**

How to Understand the Bible by Knofel Staton
   Easy-to-apply study methods and principles for the layman. This book contains step-by-step lessons, plus discussions of topics, words, customs, and contexts, to help you get the most out of Bible study. For individual or classroom use **(40046).**

The World Into Which Jesus Came by Sylvia Root Tester
   This Bible-times encyclopedia, for children in grades four through eight, explains Jewish history, laws, daily life, customs, places, and events in a comprehensive yet readable text. Hundreds of handsome full-color illustrations **(4951).**

Basic Bible Dictionary (available January 1984)
   Simplified definitions of a select list of Bible words, places, and people. A useful reading aid for children, youth, and adults, this dictionary includes words from the King James Version that have changed in meaning. Many illustrations, some in full color **(2770).**

Available at your Christian bookstore or

STANDARD
PUBLISHING